D1518341

BLACK ROCOCO

BLACK ROCOCO

RON KURZ

M. EVANS AND COMPANY, INC. / NEW YORK, N.Y. 10017

M. Evans and Company titles are distributed in
the United States by the J. B. Lippincott Company,
East Washington Square, Philadelphia, Pa. 19105;
and in Canada by McClelland & Stewart Ltd.,
25 Hollinger Road, Toronto M4B 3G2, Ontario

LIBRARY OF CONGRESS CATALOGING IN PUBLICATION DATA

Kurz, Ron.
Black Rococo

I.   Title.
PZ4.K9693Bl   [PS3561.U77]   813'.5'4   75–16278
ISBN   0–87131–196–8

Design by Joel Schick

Manufactured in the United States of America

9 8 7 6 5 4 3 2 1

SUPERDUDE DAY

SUPERDUDE DAY

Mist, tinged with the smell of bacon grease and coffee, lay over the service area parking lot, the Exxon gas pumps, and the orange-domed restaurant. A Cadillac Eldorado was parked illegally at the entrance to the restaurant. It had a leopard-skin roof and gangster whitewalls.

The two who had come in the car—a white man and a black man—were sitting inside the restaurant at a window booth. Both were busily finishing off breakfast.

It was Good Friday. It was also the beginning of spring vacation.

A bus full of children, in proper holiday spirit, was offloading in the parking lot. They were southbound. Probably Washington. To eat box lunches under cherry blossoms and trek museum corridors. For the moment though, cheering and galloping, they stormed the restaurant to buy taffy and demolish rest rooms.

Not all of them made it inside.

Some paused at the Eldorado, fingering its metal and glass, its fabric and chrome—until shooed away by the chaperons.

The two men, eyeing every movement from the booth, gulped down their coffee and stood to leave.

Superdude and Mr. Gimpelman, a short man in an expensive business suit, walked out of the restaurant. Mr. Gimpelman had paid the tab and was tucking his wallet away. Superdude, hulking and muscular, towered over the man by head and shoulders. He had to bend down to speak to him. "They recognized me in there," he said.

Mr. Gimpelman answered in a stentorian voice, all the while chomping on a cigar. "How the hell could they? I keep telling you, Lorenzo. Now how the hell could they? Public's seeing the film today for the first time."

"Ain't no jive," said Superdude. "They's staring at me. I can feel it."

"Imagination," grumbled Mr. Gimpelman. He unlocked the passenger side of the Eldorado. Superdude stood aside as if expecting the door to be opened for him. Ignoring the gesture, Gimpelman walked around to the driver's side.

A family coming from a station wagon in the parking lot stopped and gaped at Superdude with wide-eyed wonder.

"What you honkies looking at? I ain't gonna be famous till tomorrow."

The family fled inside the restaurant.

"Lorenzo," said Mr. Gimpelman. "I've told you about that. It's got to stop."

"Call me Superdude."

"Look, friend," said the little man, taking the cigar from his mouth, "just do like we decided, just try to act mysterious and dignified. And the best way to do that, Lorenzo, is to keep your mouth shut."

Superdude yanked the door open for himself and climbed in. "Well, tell those motherfuckers to stop staring at me. Ain't no reason to stare at me till tonight." He banged his head on the roof, knocking askance his chinchilla hat with the wide brim.

"God, what a screwball!" mumbled Gimpelman.

Besides the hat, Superdude also wore black leather pants, a velveteen pullover studded with rhinestones, and high-heeled cavalry boots. Wrapped about his shoulders was a full-length black cape made from the skins of an endangered species.

Mr. Gimpelman started the engine and pulled the Eldorado into the southbound exit from the service area, past the gas pumps where two towheaded young men stood with mouths agape. "Forget these people," he said, accelerating. "We've got a whole bloody city waiting for us."

In the city to the south, Superdude Day had dawned crisp and windy. Clifton Praeger, a lanky young man, showered and shaved, then showered again, trying to shake away the numbness in his limbs, the numbness of mind. He had sat awake in his apartment throughout the night. He was anxious to get to work and have the day be lived and done with.

As he was dressing, an announcement was made on the radio that Superdude was going to make an in-person appearance at the Rococo Theatre. A shiver of apprehension climbed his spine. *The Black Rococo,* he thought aloud, admonishing the announcer for his stupidity. *It's now the Black Rococo Theatre.*

Clifton Praeger was manager of the Black Rococo Theatre.

"How's it going?" asked Mr. Gimpelman, glancing sideways. The Eldorado was crossing the southbound span of the Delaware Memorial Bridge.

Superdude, sitting next to him, was mumbling to himself, rehearsing the script of his act—a brief stage appearance with a joke or two and a sweep of cape to follow each showing of *Superdude.*

"*Hey!*" yelled Mr. Gimpelman over the drone of stereophonic music. "How's it going, Lorenzo?"

"Going smooth, man." Superdude's voice was slow and static, the voice of an urban dullard. In fact, it was such a bad voice that much of the film had to be looped, using a professional.

Superdude was no professional.

Meanly handsome and street-wise, he had been plucked off a corner in Harlem. *Superdude* was his first acting experience. His real name was Lorenzo Jones. He had been paid a grand sum of $4,750 for his services in the film, which had included, among other things, the garroting of three white policemen, the submachine-gunning of seven white mobsters, the karate-chopping demise of a crooked white politico and two henchmen, besides making love (if one wished to call it that) to no fewer than five young morsels—feminine and Caucasian.

The $4,750 was more money than Lorenzo Jones had ever seen. What he didn't know at the time he signed the contract was that the seventeen-year-old stepson of the producer—a freckled kid who was to hold the sound grips at union scale during filming—would be paid more.

Lorenzo's money never saw a bank. It went with effortless dispatch to clothes, women, partying, and hangers-on. Also, he had neglected to pay income tax on the windfall and was a week away from being seriously in debt to Uncle.

With the film completed, and faced once more with unemployment lines, Lorenzo had been rescued by Mr. Gimpelman. The little man had popped up in Harlem one day, telling Lorenzo it was no less than criminal that the distributor was dumping the film without promotion.

But, he explained with much flair, he was in a position to do something about it. He could help. He talked Lorenzo into making a personal appearance. He was quite persuasive, quite understanding. Lorenzo Jones, a.k.a. Superdude, was to get fifty dollars and his meals and transportation taken care of for his efforts.

Mr. Gimpelman was general manager for a theatre chain gambling with the film. A première was scheduled in their most palatial theatre. They had gone the whole route: TV and billboards, circulars and loud-speakers, radio and newspapers. The little man estimated, with two or three shows selling out daily, he could add about twenty thousand a week to the company's coffers for his efforts—not to mention putting himself in good stead with the man who signed bonus checks.

"What's this mean here?" asked Superdude, pointing to the second page of his two-page script. " 'We aren't going to be on the wrong side of no holocaust, no more smelly end of the stick for us.' "

"What about it?"

"Well, I know what it means about the smelly end of the stick—but what's that other, them other words?"

"Holocaust?"

"Yeah, that's the one."

"God, Lorenzo, I've explained it three times. It means great destruction, like when the Jews got gassed over in Germany."

"Oh, yeah, that. But what's it mean?"

"Just say it. Don't worry about what it means. Let me worry about what it means. You just get up there and go through the routine like we agreed."

"I don't know. I feel funny in my stomach."

"Take an aspirin next stop. It'll be all right."

"How do you know so much?"

"Because, Lorenzo, I've got a small fortune tied up in you and it's *got* to be all right."

SUPERDUDE DAY

Praeger had his coffee at a drugstore near his apartment. He then waited on the corner for a downtown bus. Trash and broken bottles littered the sidewalk. Kids were out already, on bikes and skateboards, racing along the curb, defying oncoming traffic. The air was thick and oppressive, laden with toxic gases whose touch hurt the skin. Fat women waddled past carrying market bags and umbrellas. Block upon block, for as far as he could see, every second or third house stood vacant and boarded, abandoned to back taxes, stenciled NO TRESPASSING—CITY PROPERTY.

The bus he caught was crowded. He had to stand, head bent to keep from scraping the roof. Teen-agers, in holiday mood, off from classes, dominated the back with smoking and joking, giggling and cursing.

Several passengers stared at him, at his height, which always seemed exaggerated in close quarters. With a heating vent blowing hot air into his face, he scanned the bus and its mishmash of ripped seats, scrawled graffiti, and defaced ad cards. One profanity, written artfully in large Day-Glo purple at the base of the ceiling, wound out for five rows of seats.

After the Central Avenue stop, a space opened next to

a black boy in his late teens. He was sleeping with his head of furrowed cornrows against the dirty window glass. No sooner had Praeger sat down than the bus jolted. His body slammed against the boy, waking him. Immediately, angry eyes popped open, rheumy and disoriented.

"Excuse me," said Praeger.

The boy glared in return. "What's wrong with you? You crazy?"

"I'm sorry."

A huffing sound escaped the boy's mouth. He looked Praeger up and down. "Fucking white people think you own everything."

"I'm sorry," Praeger repeated.

"Sorry? What's that mean? Sorry, my ass."

Praeger said nothing.

Black youngsters nearby nudged one another, cooing in low tones. Aware of an appreciative audience, the boy's voice became boisterous, edged with bravado.

"You ugly white motherfucker. You better not get on my bus and start pushing me around, then telling me you're sorry."

Praeger stared straight ahead. He could feel his cheeks burning.

"What you looking at? You don't get on my bus like a crazy fool, then push me and look away. Who you think you are?"

"Look, fellow, I'm sorry."

"Who you calling boy?"

"I didn't say boy."

"You're the only boy I see, you punk whitey motherfucker."

Praeger, feeling all at once drained and helpless, looked at the other passengers; each wore a placard—grinning, frightful, intimidated. Everyone seemed to be expecting a sudden flailing of arms.

"Look, lad, I'm sorry I bumped you. Really, I'm sorry. What more can I say?"

"I don't want to hear no more about you being sorry. We ain't afraid of you white people no more. None of you. We're through being afraid."

"Excuse me," said Praeger, standing. "Go back to sleep. I'll find another seat."

The boy started to stand in challenge, but seeing Praeger's formidable height he changed his mind. He sat down, lowered his head, and pretended to sleep.

Praeger could feel every eye focused on him. He felt like a fool. He should have, he knew, if for no reason beyond the sheer machismo of it, punched the boy in the mouth.

Downtown, at Stricker and Emerson, Praeger got off. The boy got off also, as did most of the other blacks. He thought for a moment it was some conspiracy to challenge him in a street fight. Then he realized they were queuing up to see *Superdude.*

Superdude dozed the rest of the trip. In his mind he was mulling over the day, fantasizing about what lay ahead. Visions of all manner occupied his mind. Black, sleek women waiting for him, applauding him, throwing their arms about him, whispering seductive words, kissing him sloppily and sensuously, sticking lush breasts in his face. . . .

Gimpelman wheeled the Eldorado into the city as if it were a Roman chariot bearing Caesar.

Bounding over streets in disrepair of various stages, Superdude awoke, yawning and belching, bleary-eyed and thick-tongued, his mind still aswirl with sexual escapades. He rubbed his eyes and scratched his crotch. Then he broke into a sly smile.

"You look happy with yourself," said Gimpelman. They were passing through a ghetto neighborhood of red-brick row houses with dirty marble stoops. Beyond the houses stood gray cinder-block projects.

"Feeling okay, man," said Superdude, his smile broadening. A group of black men loitering in front of a barroom stared at the passing Eldorado with more than cursory interest.

It went that way, intersection after intersection, turned head after turned head, until they entered the downtown business district.

Swinging into Stricker Street they met a human barricade. Gimpelman slammed on the brakes. He tried to back up. It was too late. The car was immediately surrounded.

Ahead of them, beyond a sea of people, stood a massive old movie palace—Kane's Black Rococo Theatre.

"Superdude's here! Superdude's here!" voices in the crowd began squealing. Hands and noses and mouths pressed against every inch of window glass. "It's Superdude!"

Gimpelman leaned on the horn. The sound it produced was deafening—a shrill wolf whistle, extended and comical, each hullabaloo of which brought a round of applause. Finally, two mounted police came up the street and escorted them curbside of the theatre. Inching forward, Gimpelman sounded the lament once more. Those waiting for tickets broke ranks and stormed the car, pressing tight about it, palms out, clawing the glass.

"*Good God!*" stammered Superdude. "They's crazy."

"They love you, Lorenzo, they love you." Gimpelman was beaming. He brought the car to a halt and cut the ignition. "Didn't I tell you it would be the greatest, Lorenzo? Huh, now didn't I?"

"They's crazy," he repeated.

Gimpelman gave him a playful poke in the ribs. "Hey, I better start calling you Superdude."

"How we gonna get inside, man?"

Without answering, Gimpelman bounded from the car. "All right, ladies and gentlemen, clear the way! Hot stuff! Hot stuff! Superdude needs elbow room. Clear the way, folks. He's coming out."

Gimpelman raced around and opened the passenger side. Superdude began to slide out, but paused at the wall of leering faces.

"Give the man room, folks." Gimpelman turned aside and exhaled a magnanimous sigh of distress. "He's a bad mother. Don't want to see anyone hurt." He then leaned inside and hissed at Superdude. "*Give a smile. Act like you're enjoying it.*"

"I ain't enjoying it worth a fuck."

"So *act*, already, for God's sake!"

Act, act, act. . . .

The word brought back a blur of images for Superdude—memories of summer past. Klieg lights and reflectors. Cameras and sound booms. Long breaks with nothing to do. People wandering about snapping pictures with Nikkormats. Cups of coffee and sacks of juicy corned-beef sandwiches. Polite voices telling him where to stand, what to say, who to smash, who to stomp, who to blow away. And then the whispers.

Those whispers.

He can't act. Where'd they get this stiff? Can't act a lick. Christ, can't act? He can't even read the bloody script!

Everytime Lorenzo heard the whispers he thought of the money and the Scotch and milk and the fine light-skinned women he was bedding night after night. That tended to soothe his feelings. Besides, he knew the fools doing the whispering rattled to work on the IRT, whereas a Mercedes limousine picked him up each dawn at Amsterdam and 114th.

Let the motherfuckers whisper.

He remembered other whispers. When he was a kid in Alabama. His father would sneak into the house late at night and sleep on the mattress beyond the dividing sheet with his mother.

They weren't supposed to do that. County law said a family could not receive public assistance so long as a full-grown, able-bodied male inhabited the household.

It mattered not that the family consisted of nine children or that there was no work for a black man paying more than ninety cents an hour.

Not that Lorenzo's father would have taken work at ninety *dollars* an hour.

His father was an entrepreneur of no small skill. His name was Moses. Moses Jones. Although illiterate, although burdened with unusually disagreeable looks, although an alcoholic, he managed with one venture or another to avoid playing the white man's servitor. In fact, through one of his endeavors he achieved lasting renown, not to mention a namesake animal.

How many people have a namesake animal? Moses Jones had one: the Moses hare.

The Moses hare was a pink-eyed, outsize breed of rabbit that populated the western edge of the county in such numbers that hunters came from a tristate area just for the sport of shooting them dead. They were sluggish and dumb and easy prey. Their only defense was their ability to propagate.

There were thousands of them.

Lorenzo was ten years old when his father started the rabbit farm in their back lot among the discarded tires and tin cans and junk cars. Lorenzo's job was to clean out the drop pans beneath the hutches. Simple enough it seemed, yet the nature of rabbits was such that it soon became a full-time chore.

The business expanded; the half-acre of land was quickly consumed by four-tiered hutches. All went well for about a year. Then, with money in pocket, Moses Jones began spending much time away from the rabbits and more and more time hanging about the general store and liquor outlet, gin bottle in hand.

He came home besotted one October night and began cuffing Lorenzo about. It seemed the boy hadn't finished mucking the hutches before dark. Lorenzo ran out the back door crying with indignant rage.

Was it his fault that before getting to the last cage the first was again full of shit?

He pouted among the hutches for a while, among the

rising steam from the droppings, staring nose to nose at the dumb, pink-eyed things sitting there eating and shitting, getting fat, and for what? To get butchered, that's what!

Chills of claustrophobia ran through him. He put himself in their place. And he didn't like it one bit. It made him just mad enough to do something about it. He didn't much like the rabbit shit business to begin with—and the rabbit shit business was precisely what he figured he was in.

He started opening the cages and setting them free. Flipping the latches. Prodding them out. Cage after cage. Row after row.

By the time his father sobered up enough to realize what was happening, it was too late. They were everywhere. In the house. The garden. The porch. The dirt road out front. They scattered in all directions, hopping for their lives. Dogs were going berserk among them on neighboring farms, chewing them up. They even reached the state route, where cars were squashing them into the asphalt.

Moses Jones staggered about his half-acre for the next hour trying to latch hold of Lorenzo, bent on strangling him on the spot.

Lorenzo hid in a neighbor's cornfield overnight, stared at by dozens of eerie pink eyes. . . .

From that evening on, the county became known for its spectacularly good rabbit hunting and Moses Jones became known as the man who lived in the swamp so his family could get welfare.

Then, one spring day, Moses came around in broad daylight. He was God-awful tired of creeping about at night and whispering with his wife. He was going off to Detroit to make cars and get rich.

He went from child to child, bidding them farewell. Hugging and kissing them. Lorenzo was last to be approached. He didn't hug or kiss Lorenzo. Instead, he offered a few words. And the last words Lorenzo heard from his father were anything but whispered. "Boy, you ain't ever gonna amount to diddly-shit."

Never, in all his years in the red-necked South and all his later years in the streets of first Yonkers, then Harlem, had Lorenzo Jones been so scared. The people lunged and flailed at him. Tightened around him like a smothering vice. He felt helpless, being squeezed and compressed at whim, utterly at the mercy of a deranged mob.

Only once before could he remember such a horrid experience. As a young teen-ager in a rubble-filled lot— shortly after being packed off to New York to live with an "aunt"—he recalled being rolled up in a discarded, rain-soaked carpet. God, the squirming, suffocating feeling of doom when that smelly fabric enclosed him! Causing him to scream and cringe with anguish. He had felt all sanity and consciousness slipping asunder. He had a terrifying feeling of his body leaving him, of dying. And he would have too, had he not been unrolled in time by his playmates.

And now, once more, he was experiencing the exact same feeling as Gimpelman guided him through the chanting mob into the lobby of Kane's Black Rococo Theatre.

Herman Kane weighed three hundred and seventeen pounds. Once seated for the day, he rarely moved from the padded, electrically heated, reinforced swivel chair in his office. Food and newspapers were brought to him. A refrigerator was at hand.

He spent the hours between nine and five eating, reading trade papers, checking over box office statements, and taking phone calls from his demented wife.

Behind his desk was a map of the city with dozens of tiny red flags stuck in it. Forty years earlier he had started in the work world sweeping out a machine shop, and now, for each flag in his map he owned or controlled a motion picture theatre.

He had made his money in ball bearings and put it into motion picture theatres, among other ventures.

Outside the tinted windows this particular day was sunny and smoggy-pink, touched with whispers of spring. Winter was at last over.

Another money-losing winter.

The old man was spending the morning shuffling papers, swiveling in his chair, waiting for word from his general manager, Sidney Gimpelman. He was also cursing the day he had gotten out of ball bearings.

Gimpelman arrived a bit after ten. He gave a cursory knock on the office door and bounded in. "Well, boss, our friend Superdude's deposited safe and sound."

The old man pretended to be busy. He waited for Gimpelman to settle in a chair, then he looked up. "What's he like?"

"He's an idiot."

The old man cleared his throat. For some reason he was sounding like a frog to himself. "Things going like you said they would?"

"Sure. He's eager for the money. We probably could have gotten him for the price of some wine."

"You priced wine lately?" The old man coughed, dabbing his nose with a Kleenex. "So, don't just vegetate—how much to rent the Cadillac?"

"Two hundred a day."

"Nothing for security?"

"Three thousand," said Gimpelman.

"*Three thousand!* Don't those people have an insurance company? What's with a three thousand deposit?"

Gimpelman straightened his tie. "The pimp it belongs to had his lawyer there. He wanted three thousand security or no deal. So what could I do? I took care of it."

"You took care of it?" The old man flipped through some papers on his desk. "With all this Supershit advertising there's less than a thousand in the Rococo account. We're advertising our advertising. How the hell did you take care of it?"

"I wrote a personal."

"A *personal!* You got three grand to go around writing checks? I ought to cut your salary. You probably thieved it from me, anyhow."

"No way," said Gimpelman, looking at the map. "I'll wait till we're packing niggers in twenty of those theatres. Then watch out."

Herman Kane grinned.

SUPERDUDE DAY

Truck horns wailed. Blacks, swarms of them, all con-
verging on the Rococo, crossed amid morning traffic.
Praeger had just opened and already hundreds were in
line at the box office. Crowd-control poles and chains dis-
sected the sidewalk; police department traffic barriers
continued further, into the side alley. No Parking signs
hung from every meter. Mounted police patrolled Stricker
Street, clip-clopping along the curb, trying to keep the
throngs on the walk.

Illegally parked in front of the theatre was the sleek
black Eldorado with leopard-skin roof, elaborate antenna, fur seat covering, a chrome hood-mounted stallion in
a rearing stance, and gangster whitewalls.

Inside the theatre, Teddy Winkle emerged from his
office and began a search for Praeger. He was wearing an
extra-large Superdude T-shirt over his suit coat, set off
with a wide, flowered tie.

Teddy Winkle was nineteen years old, affable and hy-
peractive. Teddy Winkle was district manager for downtown theatres. Teddy Winkle shared a plush office with
the concession manager on an upper level of the Rococo.

Teddy Winkle referred to old man Kane as Uncle
Hermie.

"It's fantastic," he shouted, spotting Praeger in the front vestibule. "I love it. *I love it.* Superdude's upstairs now. People nearly tore him apart coming in. You saw it, didn't you? God. It's unbelievable. We'll do ten thousand today for sure."

Praeger said nothing. Across the vestibule, by the entrance doors, two flapping arms connected to a baggy sports coat were motioning for attention. The arms belonged to Hawkes, a young cohort of Teddy Winkle's who worked as alternate manager at the Rococo.

Hawkes' one other claim to fame was an ability to dial on the locked phones in the manager's office. Since managers weren't allowed keys to their own phones he was often called upon to perform his specialty. By rapidly depressing the receiver buttons in numerical series he was able to dial any number required, although an occasional slip of finger would produce a wrong party. He once reached Skiddy, Kansas, at the expense of Kane Theatres.

"Couple merchants just cornered me," he yelled over Clyde hats and Afros. "They're complaining about the line blocking entrances. Especially the ten-cent store. Can't nobody get in or out."

"*I love it,*" said Teddy Winkle.

"What should we do?"

"Hump them," he yelled back. "We can't do anything about the lines. We're just gonna sell tickets. Sell tickets."

"But—"

"Hide somewhere where they can't find you. Like do something useful. Like go in the box office. Yeah, get in the box office and answer the phone for Ida. She can punch tickets faster."

Piqued, Hawkes left the vestibule and entered the box office by its side door. Unattended, the area where Hawkes had been stationed immediately jammed up with in-rushing patrons. Teddy Winkle vanished into a herd of them and allowed himself to be swept away, leaving the problem to Praeger.

Praeger began mumbling to himself.

Close by, his seventy-two-year-old doorman, Brother Jason—all snow-white hair and knowing eyes and big ears decorated with warts—stood at his stand tearing tickets as fast as arthritic hands would allow. A latter-day Uncle Remus, sort of, Brother Jason was the first black person ever hired within Kane's organization above the position of charwoman. Praeger had hired him.

"That Superdude dude just sailed in, bossman. Dressed like some uptown pimp. Furry faggot cape and all. He looked scared, real scared, when all the peoples crowded at him. Mr. Gimpelman had to drag him past."

"I saw it," said Praeger, helping to tear tickets. Indeed, he had witnessed the fiasco from a side exit—one of the few doorways still safe to open. And even then, seven or eight people had approached trying to buy their way in.

"Is that true what they say?" asked Brother Jason.

"Huh?"

"That the car's got a waterbed and bar in back."

"That's what they say."

"Well—the kids is at it already."

"What do you mean? What kids?"

"Look for yourself." Brother Jason paused in his ticket ripping to motion outside. A mob along the curb had the car engulfed. They saw a boy in a flannel coat and dungarees wiggle from the crowd carrying a hubcap. Another followed with a New York license plate and a section of antenna.

"Hope Superdude brought bus fare," said Praeger.

Brother Jason grinned.

"Cliff," called Teddy Winkle from the upper concourse, "you take charge down there. All but concession. Benny's behind the stand. I'm going up to the booth to see Ledbetter about spotlights."

"What about that Superdude guy?"

"Let him stay in my office. Gimpelman'll be around when it's time for him to go on stage." Teddy Winkle disappeared once more, then his head popped back like a jack-in-the-box. "And get him anything he wants."

Brother Jason nudged Praeger. He turned in time to see an eight-year-old racing across Stricker Street with a hood ornament in hand—then, behind him, two others carrying the hood.

The ticket lines disintegrated into a mass of bodies. All order disappeared. Standee poles were pulled from sockets and tossed into the street. People jammed up six abreast at the box office: screeching housewives with babies and shopping bags, sullen teen-agers, uniformed transit workers and sad-faced laborers, retirees and school girls, winos and street thugs. All pressed forward. All thrust money at Ida Schmidt, the ninety-five-pound cashier smacking gum behind the glass.

Ida worked smoothly, methodically, trancelike, shoving big bills aside for Teddy Winkle—who had somehow joined Hawkes—to count and band. Teddy Winkle was famous that way—being where he wasn't expected.

"Going out of my mind," he chanted. "I'm going stone bananas."

Mingling with the throngs outside were high school students from the suburbs, gold and green clad, toting various horns and drums and flagstaffs, clutching tattered and betussled pieces of uniform. Unloading farther up Stricker Street, as arranged, they had tried to march in formation down to the Rococo. They never made it.

A pole crashed against the box office window. Women screamed and jumped back. The glass split into large hunks and collapsed. Hawkes fell to the box office floor —still talking into the phone. Teddy Winkle clutched bundles of money to his chest. Hands began reaching around the jagged edges. Praeger came in and stacked chairs in the opening. Calmly, Ida carried her tray of change and ticket canisters to an auxiliary window; with studied indifference she pulled the curtain, displayed her price sign, and opened once more.

Praeger returned to the lobby.

"Where's Superdude! We wants Superdude!" came a singsong voice through the front glass. "Bring out Superdude! We wants that bad dude!"

Outside, beyond the clamor of Superdude admirers, two collectors of memorabilia could be seen carrying an automobile radiator up the sidewalk, trailing severed hoses and dangling clamps. . . .

"I don't like it," said Brother Jason. "Them fools is gettin' unsettled."

Patrons began complaining of being unable to hear the soundtrack. Praeger opened the auditorium door and stuck his head inside. The place was overflowing. Aisles were jammed with patrons wandering about in search of seats. Everyone seemed to be talking at once.

The complaints were well-founded. Praeger couldn't hear the soundtrack either.

He buzzed Ledbetter in the projection booth and told him to turn the volume up a decibel or two. Ledbetter grunted and slammed the phone. Ledbetter didn't like to be disturbed in his ritual of reading the morning papers, including the *Post*, the *Sun*, the *Inquirer*, the *Times*, and the *Globe*.

Two minutes later Praeger was besieged with complaints of bursting eardrums. Ledbetter, as usual, was being difficult. Praeger buzzed the booth and asked that the sound be turned down a decibel or two.

Again, he stuck his head inside the auditorium.

Superdude, giant-size, struck with a karate chop on screen—zap, zap. A swipe at the throat and blood gushed from the victim's mouth. Zap! A chop to the groin, blood gushed forth again, buckets of it. A chop to the left elbow —same results.

The next attacker fared no better. One punch and blood bubbled from his mouth as if the poor soul was concealing a sixteen-ounce bottle of Heinz tomato ketchup in his palate.

Out front, the mob surrounding Superdude's pimpmobile began ripping door latches and chrome strips from the body. Police tried half-heartedly to stop it, but were jostled aside in the crush.

The car doors popped open. A hundred hands reached inside, tearing away sun visors, bits of upholstery, knobs and switches, carpet and seat belts.

Someone punctured the waterbed.

Bumpers went, then the headlights and wipers, then the trunk lid. Two middle-aged men in work clothes produced a jack to hoist the back up. Water sloshed forward, covering the TV and bar and instrument panel. The men pulled the rear tires off and rolled them up Stricker Street. A band of teen-age urchins immediately took up the crusade and, with much supervision from the would-be mechanics among them, removed the front tires.

Praeger made his way to the upstairs office. Opening the door, he found an argument in full bloom between Gimpelman and Superdude.

Superdude was crouched in the corner behind Teddy Winkle's file cabinets, a cape pulled over his head. All the while, Gimpelman was bantam-hopping about the office, shaking his fist.

"Lorenzo, you can't do this! You can't throw this opportunity away. . . ."

"I'm Superdude."

"What did you say?"

"Call me Superdude."

Gimpelman's face seemed to billow like some exotic bird fluffing plumage. "Look, you asshole, you know how much we've put out for promotion? You think all of this comes for nothing? And you're sitting there telling me you're not going on. Look, don't pull that prima-donna crap on me, Lorenzo, you hear, not Gimpelman. You're not with your sporting crowd now, you hear?"

"I ain't going out in front of them savages," Superdude mumbled.

"*Savages!* What kind of talk is that? They're your own flesh and blood people. . . ."

Praeger cleared his throat, drawing their attention.

"What the hell do you want?" said Gimpelman, snapping his head toward the door.

Superdude peeped from beneath his cape. "My man," he said, straightening somewhat, looking at Praeger, "I could use a drink."

"Water fountain's downstairs."

"Praeger, Goddamnit! What the hell do you want?" repeated Gimpelman.

"I only came to tell you about that shitwagon out front."

"So what about it?"

"Nothing left but the frame."

Uncomprehending, Gimpelman stared at him for an instant. "Oh my God!" he murmured, bursting past Praeger. "*Oh my God!*" He charged from the office, bounding down the Grand Staircase and across the lobby, pushing people aside with both arms. When he reached the street he met a wall of black youths waiting for tickets. He tried to plow through them, but they held fast—before hitting back. They knocked him to the ground with the tape-wrapped sticks they carried. His shoes and necktie were ripped off and thrown into the crowd. A boy with cornrowed hair picked the wallet from his clothing, all the while screaming profanities, pounding with his stick.

Using his telephone specialty, Hawkes called an ambulance.

SUPERDUDE DAY

"Fuck you, man! I ain't going out there," said Superdude, still behind the file cabinet.

Praeger could feel his stomach turning somersaults; he could feel spittles of saliva flying out as he spoke. "You've got to go on!"

"I ain't gotta do nothing."

"The audience'll tear the walls down," said Praeger, his voice pleading. "It'll be a holocaust with all these people inside."

Superdude's eyes flickered. "I know what that means," he said.

"Huh?"

"It means big destruction, don't it?"

"Oh, yes, definitely yes," said Praeger.

Superdude was quiet for a moment. "It means too," he said finally, "that Superdude ain't fool enough to get his head beat in—like the number your boss just got done on his."

"Gimpelman'll be all right. Guy driving the ambulance said so."

"What's that fool know? I seen dudes that was bleeding to death smile at you stepping into the ambulance."

"Gimpelman wasn't smiling."

28

Superdude scratched his left buttock and pulled the cape completely over his head, shroudlike. "I heard all about it once, man. And I don't wants to hear it no more."

Praeger looked at his watch. The feature had but a few minutes to run. Then the lights would go on. Following which, as advertised, Superdude was expected on stage. In person.

Thinking about it, Praeger was beginning to have doubts about the future of his own well-being.

"M'man," Superdude whispered from beneath the cape. "You got to help me get to the bus station. . . ."

"*Like shit!*" Praeger went to him and began tugging on his sequined pullover. "You're going on stage!"

"Leave off me, honky-tonk."

Praeger backed away. "There's a magnum revolver downstairs says you're going on."

"Shee-it! You ain't gonna shoot nobody. . . ."

"Watch me," said Praeger.

He went to the door and cracked it enough to look out. Immediately he was sorry. Flesh filled the gap. Fingers and elbows stuck through the sliver of an opening. He pushed back with all his might.

The people weren't trying to get in, he realized—instead, they were being shuffled and crushed against the woodwork in the rampage across the upper concourse. He looked again. Tiers of bodies were backed up on the Grand Staircase. Hundreds of blacks were jamming the balcony entranceways, pushing and struggling to get a view of the stage, a view of Superdude's entry.

Chanting drifted up from the auditorium. The ending credits were showing on screen. The singsong reverberating through the building was infectious.

Superdude, Superdude, we wants Superdude!

Praeger shut the door. He looked at his watch. It was showtime. Tiny white explosions peppered his vision. *Oh, Jesus,* he mumbled to himself, staring at the sweep of the second hand, *what am I doing here?*

Clifton Praeger was just recently twenty-nine years old.

At twenty-four he had been caught in an attempt to avoid the draft. It was an ill-fated effort from the start, consisting of college, a green-eyed wife, a city row house, and a quire of shifting, nebulous Selective Service regulations. It ended with him being conscripted into the Army.

He went to Vietnam as an infantryman.

Toward the end of his tour he was wounded. Seriously. He spent more than a year in various hospitals. Eventually —sutures faded, shattered bone mended, able to maneuver without crutch or cane—he was discharged.

33

Returning home, he used his B.A. and his veteran's pref-
erence to become a caseworker for a city agency.

Although he had not the slightest calling for social
work, he awoke each morning knowing the day's hassle
would provide one hundred and seventy-three dollars at
week's end for his thirty-seven and one-half hours.

Before long, though, he found himself in a dilemma:
bills to be paid each week, yet each week an urge to run
screaming from those offices and never return.

He was unable to play his employers' game. He couldn't
keep up the required façade of officialdom; he couldn't
turn himself on and off like a light switch—not after en-
countering the pathetic people in his case load: the reclu-
sive old women living on dog food, the arthritic with
swollen scabby limbs, the friendless blind and slobbering
senile. . . .

It seemed as if every despairing, malodorous, bedrid-
den creature about the city lurked in his cabinet of manila
folders. God, he came to hate it.

Yet he went out each morning.

Soon he was doing more and more for his charges—
much more than required by interview and fill-in-the-
blank session—and less paper-shuffling and water-fountain
politicking (a development much opposed to the thinking of his superiors, the department, the city, and his
own better judgment). He found himself running errands
for a legless, wart-covered old man. He found himself
reading stories to a young girl who lived alone and had a
flipperlike thing growing out of her side. He found himself unsticking windows, putting up shelves, unclogging
toilets. He found himself shopping for groceries and picking up medicine—usually refusing reimbursement.

He was always behind in his office work, yet he could do the job no other way. He began staying past the five o'clock quitting time. He began making visits on weekends, on his own time. Once, he took his green-eyed wife along, but it turned out disastrously: they discovered the client dead and rotting in scummy bathtub water.

After that day his wife never wanted to hear a word about his work. She refused to show the slightest interest in the plight of his charges, or in him.

He began working later into the evenings, and more often on weekends. And he continued giving away much of his pay.

The marriage collapsed.

He quit his job in an effort to make things right, but it was too late. He remembered when they separated (her idea), she had—benign soul that she was—packed him a "going away" box to outfit his newly acquired, depressingly furnished apartment. The box contained one knife, one spoon, one fork, and one chipped guaranteed-not-to-chip stoneware plate.

"What if I have a guest?" he asked.

"Let the pig eat with her fingers."

So goes the way of love, he thought at that instant, crushed and remorseful, *the years of heartfelt tenderness, of sacrifice and hope, as we trip the light fantastic on our journey through life. . . .*

How poetic.

She got the house, the car, the furniture, and the dog; he got one knife, one spoon, one fork, and one chipped stoneware plate.

It was a grand delusion, he suspected—this posturing

he had done as the concerned do-gooder. *Shit!* he thought, *shit!* Fact was, he just allowed himself to be talked into things too easily. His case load had been manipulating *him*. They had become victims of society; he had become their victim.

Good that he had finally quit. He was much too soft-of-heart—or soft-of-brain, whichever—for the job. Yet, his options were quickly narrowing. The military had been a horrid fiasco. The academic world was beyond him. He was too conscience-stricken for what went on in business, too lazy for everyday labors—and a bit too bungling or gullible, or both, for all between.

In short, Clifton Praeger was a fuckup.

It wasn't one of the better times in his life. The meager funds scraped up by cashing in insurance policies were gone. He was living a bologna and peanut butter existence. Two nights a week he did janitorial work; he also worked in a restaurant, washing things.

What he needed, he figured, was to be away from people, away from bureaucracies. He needed some solitary craft to inspire and consume him. No guilt feelings, no despair, no pain. No hassle. Merely some noble work to hold out front, to be prideful of, to carve every decision around.

If only he could find it.

Following the split-up with green eyes, Praeger had fled to a Bohemian neighborhood bordering Godward University. It was called Guinness Village. The spring term had just ended. Apartments were going begging at bargain rates.

Then, soon after settling in an old brownstone on St. James Street, he met a girl in Guinness Park. She was holding in her arms the ugliest puppy imaginable. The poor creature was covered with sores and its eyes were swollen and it had but a scattered patch or two of hair.

Its name was Baldy.

"I have to be careful," the girl said. "He whimpers if I pet too hard."

Praeger said nothing. They were sitting in a mottled spring haze, on a bench, watching a gang from Godward twirling frisbees to one another. The girl was very pretty. Her underarms, he noticed, were unshaven—which made her no less pretty to him.

"Had him long?" Praeger asked, reaching out and letting the puppy lick his hand.

"Found him this morning. In an alley behind Domingo Street. He was trying to turn a garbage can over."

Praeger felt his heart going out, but quickly, with the

fall of a mental guillotine, he cut it short. The pain caused by green eyes was still in his chest and he could do without complicating it.

"I've got to get him to a vet," she said. "I just brought him here to get some sunshine and fresh air. You know. The vet's going to cage him for sure. I just wanted him to know there're some good things in being alive—like parks and all, you know, instead of right from an alley to a cage. . . ."

He observed the girl until she glanced away, brushing long mahogany hair from her face. She sat Baldy in the sunshine and rummaged through a knit bag slung over her shoulder. "Cigarette?" she offered.

"No, thanks."

Her attire conformed with the uniform of the day— cut-off jeans faded pale and tight about her flanks, sandals and spoon rings, flowered cotton blouse and obvious lack of bra.

Praeger made no effort to light her cigarette. He knew her breed well enough. He'd no doubt get his hand bit if he tried.

The girl, whose name was unknown to Praeger, seemed to sense his reluctance; it appeared to please her. "Come here often?" she asked.

"No."

"I do. It's my Walden Pond."

"You make a habit of this?" asked Praeger.

"*Pardon?*"

"Picking up strays."

"Sure," she said, ducking a loose frisbee. "If they're pathetic enough."

Praeger smiled.

They were quiet for a moment, watching romping dogs and lacrosse players invading from farther up the hill. Another frisbee sailed past. "Baldy, you stay close," she said to the puppy. "This place is getting lethal."

Deliberately, as if some decision had been made, some option offered and accepted, Praeger faced her. "You go to Godward?"

She nodded her head.

"Got classes this afternoon?"

"No."

"What does one do when one leaves one's Walden Pond?" he asked, voice mocking.

"One finds a place to relieve one's bladder."

Praeger managed a smile. It seemed his new friend—besides a pixie face and frolicking fawn eyes—possessed boundless wit. "And then?"

"Baldy goes to the vet," she said, flicking ashes onto his shoes. "Hey, did you know Fitzgerald lived in those apartments across the street? Like back in the thirties."

"Who?"

"F. Scott Fitzgerald, shithead."

"Didn't know that."

"Wrote *The Crack-Up* shortly afterward."

"It figures." Praeger settled back on the bench, tucking both hands under his belt. Their knees touched momentarily, parted, then joined once more.

"What do you do?" she asked.

"I'm sort of between things. Kind of looking for something."

"Like what?"

Praeger paused before speaking. "Something away from people. I seem to mess up too much around people. . . ."

"That's interesting. How do you get by? Shit! Stupid question. You don't, right?"

"Right."

Her eyes brightened; he loved her eyes. "Hey, like look," she said, "maybe you'd be interested . . . I mean, if you're really desperate, I might be able to help. I work nights as a cashier for this rinky-dink theatre chain. They always need managers."

Praeger shook his head. "I don't know. . . ."

"Give them a call. What can it hurt?" Suddenly she stood. The noonday chimes had begun sounding from Godward. "I've got to go," she said.

"Mind if I tag along?"

She smiled, picking up Baldy. "My strays always tag along."

Praeger stood also. Without speaking, they walked together through itchy foliage and arthritic branches, emerging from the park by the art museum, then they crossed Rembrandt Street and strolled between once-palatial apartment buildings toward St. James.

"What are you thinking?" asked the girl, whose name turned out to be Michele.

"About that job. What's a theatre manager do, anyhow?"

"Unlocks doors."

He applied and got the job. A promising opportunity, he decided. Better than scrubbing pots and pans, better than cleaning toilets in office buildings—two positions with which he had become all too familiar.

The area's foremost theatre chain needs aggressive managers, the ad in the paper had said. *Be trained by experts in the field.*

The training by experts consisted of spending one evening swapping war stories with the salt-and-pepper-haired manager of the Eagle Theatre—a kindly veteran of the big war—at the bar of the Golden Apple Lounge. Quite drunk, they went back to the theatre at midnight and locked the doors.

Then they returned to the Golden Apple.

Next day Praeger was given the keys to the Rococo, a crumbling monster of a theatre on Stricker Street. He was on his own.

A revival of De Mille's *The Ten Commandments* was playing (Edward G. Robinson running around like Mr. Big in drag and Charlton Heston parting split-process waters on some studio parking lot). Praeger had small chance to watch it. Problems galore faced him as manager.

All the help he had inherited were crooks. It was remarkable, he felt, to have such an assortment of ticket-palming artists under one dome. One by one he began tripping them up and firing them. None seemed to care. They had, obviously, long since bankrolled theirs and were merely waiting out the inevitable. Finally he was down to Ida Schmidt, a wrinkled and rouged cashier, twenty-three years in the box office. Upon being caught, she burst into tears in his office, soon babbling about her own integrity and the general rottenness of the rest of the world. She was honest, she explained, when honest managers were running the place and dishonest (to keep her job, she said) when dishonest managers were in charge. It seemed that lately, she told him, there had been a long run of the latter.

Praeger, always the sucker for petticoat tears, told her she could stay.

To replace the others he called the Over-Sixty Agency and Hire The Handicapped. Within a week, after some of the most bizarre interviews imaginable, the place looked like a home for the decrepit and disfigured—but the ticket-palming ceased.

Praeger soon found himself involved with Michele, the girl he'd met in the park. She eventually moved away from her two roomies and into his lair on St. James Street. Despite her being a bit flighty, a bit smart-mouthed, and much too Sagittarian in her traits, they co-existed with remarkable ease—even out of bed. The reason being, no doubt, that they rarely saw one another in the light of day.

In addition to her studies at Godward and her cashiering downtown, Michele was continually pursuing some humanitarian crusade or another—gory things about baby seals and harpooned whales. Or, when she wasn't collecting petition signatures, she was collecting stray animals to share their bed. An irritating practice at best, but Praeger grew to love her for it, even if he could only guess at what would be licking his face in the mornings.

Baldy had been put in the care of a veterinarian for a drawn-out period of treatment for mange, among a myriad of lesser disorders. The vet had wanted to put him to sleep. He thought the case incurable. But Michele, forever quick-witted, convinced him that there was a new treatment discovered by a doctor in New York. She told him the doctor was a long-term friend and she would have him telephone. That evening she called her family's M.D. at his Long Island home and pleaded that he go along with the lie. After twenty minutes' worth of toll charges, and a lecture on medical ethics, he finally agreed. *For your father, little Miss Chutzpah, for your father, God rest his soul.* He would consult with a golf partner —who was also head of a veterinary school—and have *him* make the call. It was probably hopeless, he explained, as hopeless as her, but all his best wishes went to Baldy.

So, it ended up costing Michele thirty-five dollars a week, plus medication (an arsenic compound mixed with some mumbo-jumbo neither she, nor the vet for that matter, could decipher). By neglecting frills, and with Praeger chipping in a time or two, she managed to get it together each payday.

The months passed quickly, pleasantly; summer into fall.

On scheduled workdays Praeger would bathe in the early afternoon, soaking until the water cooled, then shower off, dry in the luxury of thick towels, and shave his face with fastidious attention. Michele insisted he was the most narcissistic bastard she'd ever seen.

He had only two suits. He took marked care with them, keeping them pressed and on hangers—and away from animal hair. He alternated between the two, never showing up in the same one on consecutive days. And he learned how to disguise and compliment each with bright ties and patterned shirts.

Occasionally, standing in the lobby, he received a compliment on his appearance. It would make him feel good for a while. But a breath away, invariably, would come a complaining grimalkin, face askance, glaring up at him with umbrella cocked.

The complaints were usually valid.

Praeger got used to hearing them. You had to get used to hearing complaints if you worked for Kane Theatres.

Kane Theatres hovered perpetually on the threshold of bankruptcy. Business was disastrous. Ever since some redneck-for-hire shot Martin Luther King and the subsequent looting of twelve thousand liquor stores, few people considered "doing downtown" very entertaining.

The city's population—poor, ethnic, black, hippie, each to their own enclave or ghetto—were into things other than moviegoing. Like survival. The would-be patrons were elsewhere, living the American Dream, surrounding the city like an asbestos inner tube, besmogging and parasitic by day, retreating in 390 cubic inches of glory at sundown.

The American Dream had its own cinemas: cinderblock boxes in shopping centers.

Of the city's dozen or so old-time movie palaces only the Rococo, the Eagle, the Granada, and the Belvedere remained—and rumor continually had one or another of them slated for parking space.

Kane's downtown operation had become a curse to the old man. And the Rococo, the largest theatre in the state, crumbling and grotesquely ornate, maintenance-prone, costly to heat and staff, felt the brunt of his ire.

Unscheduled bank deposits were demanded by ominous voices, mystically vague, calling from that magic land of Oz known as the front office. Nervous calls inquired about receipts. Terse commands were relayed: "Mr. Kane wants all your money brought up here by one o'clock, everything, your working bank, quarters, nickels, pennies, everything!" "Don't let the gas and electric meter reader in." "Lay off all ushers. Right away. Lay them all off!"

Occasionally, the check machine would "break" on payday. A rash of these calls would precede its restoration to order.

Praeger was unconcerned. He was content to be working regularly—even at one-ten a week—and was not about to be annoyed by a tardy paycheck now and again.

Besides, if he quit in a pique, what would happen to his new regiment of forlorn friends—those downtrodden urban cretins he had begun taking in (against his better judgment) as easily as Michele would a stray cat? Where would they go?

Christ, where would *he* go!

With winter approaching, he realized he was over his head. Yes, *again!* An unnerving sense of déjà vu weighed on his mind. He was once more playing the fool—a rerun of his days as Mr. Super Social-Do-Good.

Suddenly, all manner of people were beginning to depend on him. All bubbling with problems. All wanting some human warmth or kind gesture, or shelter, or money. What could he do? Turn them away? Maybe later. Maybe when spring came he would break it off and rehabilitate himself. Take the cure. But not in winter. He didn't have the heart to do it in winter.

It would wait.

Not having a left arm, Harry Harp looked at the watch on his right arm. "He'll be here," he said. The Umbrella Lady pulled her pea coat tight about her neck and grunted. Brother Jason shuffled his feet on the sidewalk. He was the only black man among them and he had rhythm.

The Button Man stood apart from them all, smiling. A bitter, midmorning wind swept Stricker Street. The Button Man seemed not to notice.

"We're due on screen in three minutes," said Ledbetter, the projectionist, looking up from a tabloid with a picture of a two-headed baby on the front. "We'll be behind schedule if we ain't on screen in three minutes."

"He'll be here," said Harry Harp.

"He gonna be late," said Brother Jason, tapping his toes. "He probably think it Hawkes' day to open."

"Nobody's seen Mr. Hawkes all week," said Debbie, the matinee concession girl.

The Umbrella Lady started to sob. Ledbetter nudged Harry Harp. "What's her problem?"

"Praeger lets her in on cold days."

"I'm cold," said Debbie.

"Hell with this waiting," said Ledbetter. "I'm going

around to Bickford's for coffee. It ain't in my contract to stand out front."

"He'll be here," said Harry Harp.

The Button Man sat down on the sidewalk and rested his back against the theatre's façade. He was still smiling.

A man in tattered clothes walked up with a slip of paper in his hand. He gave it to Ledbetter. Ledbetter looked officious.

The man mumbled something. Ledbetter read the paper and shook his head.

"He ain't here yet," said Harry Harp, seeming to know what it was about. The man took the paper back and stood against the wall, out of the wind. He had no coat, only a flannel shirt buttoned at the neck.

The Umbrella Lady screeched once, hyenalike, then paced back and forth in front of the curtained box office.

Debbie's nose began to run. She sniffled and wiped it on her scarf. Another man, this one in need of a shave, walked up, also holding a slip of paper. He conferred quietly with the first man.

"Why's the Mission House send men to Praeger?" asked Ledbetter, looking at Harry Harp. "What goes on around here, anyhow?"

"Mr. Praeger takes them in."

"Takes them in? Takes them in *where?*"

"Inside the theatre," said Harry Harp. "When the Mission House is full up they send them to Mr. Praeger."

Ledbetter's expression grew nonplussed.

Ida Schmidt joined the group. She chewed her gum and seemed unconcerned that by the clock above Kresge's there remained but a minute until showtime.

A few old ladies began to gather about the box office. "He'll be here," said Harry Harp.

"I'm cold," said Debbie.

Brother Jason tapped his toes, doing a bit of soft shoe, then, triumphantly, gestured up Stricker Street.

Praeger was approaching at a trot. His coat was open and his tie was flapping in the wind. He grinned as he drew near, jangling keys in an out-thrust hand.

"Told you he'd be here," said Harry Harp.

Without breaking stride, Praeger unlocked the front entrance, went through the vestibule, unlocked the manager's office, crossed the lobby, unlocked the concession stand, then continued to a wall panel where he began throwing light switches.

The employees filed in and scattered. The two transients remained in the vestibule with their slips of paper, looking a bit disconcerted. The old ladies waited outside for the box office to open.

"Your girl friend lock herself in the bathroom again, Mr. Praeger?" asked Brother Jason.

"No, no," he answered, racing into the manager's office to open the safe. "She set the kitchen afire cooking breakfast."

The Umbrella Lady entered the auditorium. The Umbrella Lady attended Kane's Rococo Theatre most every day. Holidays included. She had a Gold Pass, frayed and smudgy under cracked lamination—the only one Praeger had ever seen. Showing a valid Gold Pass gave the bearer admittance to any Kane Theatre at any time. It was quite a prestigious bit of cardboard. And no one could figure out how The Umbrella Lady came to possess it. Some speculated she was old man Kane's mother. Praeger didn't believe it. There was little resemblance. Besides, The Umbrella Lady's pass was expired by a decade.

She was always dressed up in black silks and a navy pea coat with all manner of rings and bracelets attached to her extremities. She wore a Tyrolean hat with a plume. She also wore a bright-orange life jacket strapped to her back. She always carried three umbrellas and a shopping bag stuffed with rain gear.

She was hydrophobic—the mental kind where you don't foam at the mouth.

Every day she would complain to Praeger, scene by scene, about how *stupide* the film had been. *Stupide*. *Stupide*. She would wave one or more of her umbrellas in his face while complaining.

In Bickford's cafeteria around the corner she was known as The Garbage Lady. She would sit down in front of deserted, half-eaten meals and finish them off.

The Button Man stayed outside in the cold waiting for the box office to open. Like The Umbrella Lady, he was also a regular. Whenever the weather was raw or he grew weary of the street or the kids taunted too much, he would pay his way into the Rococo with stacks of quarters and sit in the middle seat of the very front row. Sometimes he saw the featured picture half a dozen times. He never seemed to care. His memory was short.

He wore the same baggy clownlike pants and ragged jacket every day. Pickings of all sort protruded from his pockets—newspapers, dropped gloves, pop bottles, folded bags, discarded wrappings. His clothes were his place of business; the junk he picked up was just a sideline. His clothes were peppered with colorful tin buttons. Words were written on the buttons.

Kiss Me U Fool, Keep on Truckin, Black is Beauteous, God is Love, Makin Bacon, FCK—The Only Thing Missing is You! . . .

The Button Man had hundreds of them, head to foot.

Zip-A-Dee Doo-Dah, Gay Power, Jesus Freak, Love Me or Leave Me—Preferably Leave Me.

A quarter each.

After rock shows he would stand rotating like a card rack in front of the Municipal Center surrounded by dozens of picking and pawing kids, unpinning their choices, dropping coins into his palm.

How's Your Firn?

It was said that The Button Man had been coming into the Rococo for decades—even before The Umbrella Lady —even to the early days of Mr. Max, a famous entrepreneur and manager in the twenties and thirties who had gone crazy and left the business. Mr. Max had tried to integrate the theatre's audiences. "The shows at the Rococo are for *all* the people of our city," he had said in a press interview in 1938. Shortly afterward the rumors started that he was crazy.

Save a Tree—Eat a Beaver.

Praeger remained in the box office to watch Ida Schmidt count her bank, thread her tickets, and pull the faded curtain. Then he left her to her gum smacking and entered the lobby. The feature was just going on screen. He checked his watch.

Two minutes late.

He unlocked the remaining front doors and sent the transients to the men's room to shave and wash up. He then took the exit keys from their hook above his office pay phone and dispatched Harry Harp to unchain the balcony and auditorium exits. Brother Jason popped in and handed him a note that had been taped to the doorman's stand; it was from Dewey, the man who cleaned the theatre. A semi-illiterate scrawl informed him that something "funny" was going on backstage and that Dewey wasn't about to go back there anymore for any reason whatsoever.

Something funny was going on everywhere—to Dewey's mind at least. Some days the theatre was so hysteria-provoking it wasn't even touched.

Something funny, indeed.

He'd have a look for himself. He could use a good laugh. He took a flashlight from the office and crossed the carpeted surface of speckled cigarette burns that was called the main lobby.

Above him, cobwebs hung from gilt chandeliers. Ornamental water fountains and jardinières stood chalky dry, full of wrappers and butts. Lights were burned out, smoky and gray, crusted with insect specks. Brass railings were sea-green.

At the end of the lobby stood the concession stand with its gurgling drink dispensers and popcorn warmer and shelves of dusty candy—everything appearing permanently welded by the mucilage of decades. Crumbling stucco walls reached to the ceiling behind it, scarred and initialed, obscenity answered with obscenity.

It was painfully obvious that Kane Theatres ordered

no supplies, performed no maintenance, contracted for no cleaning, other than that required to keep an image on screen.

Praeger went up the Grand Staircase to the balcony. Four levels of climbing to survey nine hundred empty seats—minus a dozen or so that had been ripped apart by zealous patrons and never replaced. Forty years earlier Brenograph clouds had floated across the atmospheric ceiling amid sparkling, minuscule stars. But in recent times, he knew, all the audience got was an occasional droplet of water on stormy days.

Along the west wall of the balcony he pushed aside a space of heavy curtain. Dust billowed about his legs. He tried several switches on the wall. None worked. There was a black door, which he opened, then a platform emptying into a rickety stairway—the threshold of a domain which, alone, he had discovered and mapped in memory, exploring secret hallways and passages, crawlspaces and catwalks, weaving level to level, balcony to stage. No one else connected with the Rococo, it seemed, had his Taurian taste for adventure. No one else had his Herculean sense of history. No one else cared a rat's ass.

It was his hiding place, *his* Walden Pond, when the core of his being screamed for peace.

Kicking crusted paint cans and discarded bulbs, he felt along a handrail, gingerly descending the stairs, emerging at last backstage among rows of boarded and locked dressing rooms.

Chest-high heaps of official-looking papers from pre-Kane days surrounded him; financial records, canceled checks, ad proofs, 8 x 10 glossies, clippings, press releases, all dumped from storage so their filing cabinets could be used elsewhere.

Yet something was different this time. A certain *order* inhabited the mess. Wading through the debris he looked closer. Some neatly stacked items stood to the side. They were sorted by date. Others were bundled and tied, as if awaiting movement. Something funny's going on, he thought. *He* sure as hell hadn't done it.

Then he remembered Dewey's note. He pulled it from his pocket and read it again.

Sometin funny go on backstage.

III

STRANGE HAPPENINGS

SUPERDUDE DAY

A fluid movement of bodies—the transient mass remaining without seats—wove through the lobby and hallways, up stairs, in and out of lavatories. Couples, many with children in tow, soon abandoned the search and flopped on carpeted steps to smoke cigarettes, to eat smuggled pork chops and Colonel Sander's Kentucky-fried chicken. Those wanting to purchase food found it all but impossible to get near the concession stand. Passageways were often clogged, people edging through as if in fetters, stepping over one another, stumbling, cursing. There was much tussling and shoving. Skirmishes were breaking out. . . .

And beyond it all the chant continued: *Superdude, Superdude, we wants Superdude!*

Praeger left the upstairs office and elbowed his way to the Grand Staircase. Below, in front of the ladies' lounge, he could see a line of grim-faced women. One of their number, watching him as he watched her, lifted her dress and squatted by the soda machine.

"I don't believe it," he mumbled to himself.

The announced demise of Superdude, he realized, would have to wait. Much as he regretted the delay.

He maneuvered down the Grand Staircase, between the flow of bodies, uncertain of every footfall. Other people's shoes seemed to be the only thing he was stepping on. Then, at the bottom, an arm grabbed him. A husky voice demanded, "Where's Superdude, man?"

"He'll be on, he'll be on," Praeger found himself babbling. "It's only a short delay. No problem. Couple a minutes . . . to get things straight. . . ."

He was such a pathetic liar.

"Superdude better do his number, man. Else we's gettin' money back one way the other. You dig?"

Pulling away, Praeger struggled across the lobby toward his office door. Others began to pursue. "A couple minutes, only a couple minutes . . ." Angry faces crowded him. He had trouble getting the keys from his pocket. "Only a couple . . . that's all, really. Let me get the door open. Only a couple minutes."

Entreating and pleading, he managed to squeeze in. He bolted the door behind himself and backed against it for a moment, exhausted, heart pounding, finally slumping into a chair. His breathing came in short gasps. His eyelids pressed shut. Outside, he could hear fists hammering on wood. "Where's Superdude, motherfucker! We wants Superdude!"

He opened his eyes and looked down at his hands. They were trembling. Tiny red blotches covered them. He turned away and deposited a dime in the pay phone on the wall, and, knowing the city police would never come (he had once banished them for all time from the Rococo), dialed the security agency used by Kane Theatres.

His voice quavered as he spoke. "We need help," he kept repeating into the mouthpiece. "Send help."

Benny Lebowitz, concession manager and—on this frozen night soon before Christmas—acting district manager, popped his head in the office doorway. "Cliffie, baby!"

Praeger looked up, meeting a whiff of garlic.

"What's wrong, Cliffie, baby? You're awful quiet lately."

"Nothing, Mr. Lebowitz. Absolutely zilch."

Benny Lebowitz, a rotund man given in middle years to wearing gaudy sport coats and floral ties, disappeared into the lobby, creeping across the carpet in an attempt to sneak up on the teen-age girl working his stand. Catching one reading a magazine or otherwise inattentive signaled a tirade—complete with flailing arms and strained breathing—concerning the thousands of dollars of lost business these ungrateful little bitches cost him. It didn't matter that only seven patrons were in the theatre, and three of those were cat-napping policemen.

Praeger often thought it was a sexual thing with Benny Lebowitz.

In his cocoon of an office, Praeger sat back from the desk—his legs being too long to fit underneath—staring for a moment in the direction of clipboards, schedules, and directives posted on the paint-peeling wall.

There's no business like show business, indeed, indeed, indeed. . . .

Outside, the downtown streets and stores were deserted —a ghost city of the future, red and luminous under holiday ornamentation. Only the Rococo was open on Stricker Street. Its orange bulbs pulsated about the marquee, outlining the masks of Comedy and Tragedy—a beacon drawing all humanity within its portals, making it laugh, making it weep.

Unfortunately, only two specimens of humanity were in sight: a darksome dude draped in furry pelts wandering tipsily about the street and a young policeman—the lookout for the others—inside the foyer rubbing his hands, listening to static on his walkie-talkie.

Benny Lebowitz returned to the office. His face was flushed and his breathing labored. Praeger had just finished closing out the box office and was occupied with the evening statement of receipts.

"Eighty dollars I was short last week," said Lebowitz. "Just one theatre. *Eighty dollars.* That girl's robbing me blind. Robbing me blind. I don't make that kind of commission to be hustled by some molasses-ass with sticky fingers. . . ."

"Set up an inventory."

Lebowitz gave him a dirty look.

"Make the girl accountable," Praeger continued with indifference, the stock comment for Lebowitz's stock soliloquy.

"Don't have time, Cliffie baby. You know that. You see what I'm up against."

"I'd find time."

"Can't do it. Not with four theatres to look after."
Lebowitz lowered himself into a chair across the desk
from Praeger, scattering a fistful of bills from his pocket.
"Don't get me wrong, I'd like to—really and truly."

Praeger felt an urge to laugh.

Lebowitz began heaving as he counted; then, realizing he could be seen from the lobby, he nudged Praeger.
"How about closing the door for me, Cliffie baby."

"You say something, Mr. Lebowitz?"

The rotund man mumbled a profanity or two under
his breath. He shifted his bulk and yelled into the lobby:
"Cindy! Come here, Cindy! Right now. *Now.*"

A skinny, blonde-haired girl appeared. Her sweater
sleeves were rolled up and she was holding a damp
cloth. "Yes, sir," she said.

"Shut the door for me, Cindy."

"Yes, sir." The girl shut the door and left.

Slowly, Praeger looked up from his paperwork. "People
sitting in there paid three bucks a ticket, Mr. Lebowitz.
They want a three-dollar apocalypse, not—"

"Screw them old biddies."

"Look, Mr. Lebowitz . . ."

"Okay, okay, Cliffie baby, I won't yell. It's your theatre.
You're manager. If it'll make you happy I won't yell.
Okay. There. I'm not yelling."

"It'll make me happy if you stop calling me Cliffie
baby."

Lebowitz worked for 10 per cent of the concession
receipts. A vending company supplied the confections
—dyed popcorn, syrupy fruit punch, the usual assortment
of candies and nuts. Lebowitz managed. Lebowitz's man-

aging consisted mostly of hiring and firing little girls and counting money.

The girls' salaries came from his commission. Each week he would pocket an amount from one of the theatre stands, blame it on the girl, fire her, hire another. Sixteen-year-olds at a dollar-fifteen an hour were his specialty.

The phantom losses worked well at tax time.

He had other devices. Praeger made a game of figuring them out. One involved popcorn. The vending company supplied three sizes of cups for buttered popcorn: forty, fifty, and ninety-nine cents. Lebowitz posted only the fifty- and ninety-nine-cent prices on his board, sold the forty-cent cups for fifty cents, hid the fifty-cent cups, and pocketed a dime on each sale.

There were others. Jewels of ingenuity. Some that Praeger remembered as a kid. Some as old as the first Bijou.

Turning off the air conditioning, placing out-of-order signs on the water fountains, over-salting popcorn—all to spur soda sales. Then giving more ice than soda.

Barring outside food and drink.

Short dipping butter.

Displaying large candy boxes in a machine which delivered puny ones.

But Lebowitz went further. Bait-and-switch was child's play for him. For every old chestnut, Lebowitz had a half-dozen new schemes afoot, as crass and devious as the roly-poly man himself.

Lebowitz was a genius.

12

SUPERDUDE DAY

Hawkes walked in on Praeger from the adjoining box office, catching him phone in hand. A frightful look broached his face when he overheard the conversation.

The Cadillac All-Star Protective Agency offered an hourly rate fifty cents lower than competition and, therefore, was subscribed to whenever the front office decided a situation showed signs of deteriorating into a donnybrook or worse. However, managers were not allowed in on the decision-making of what constituted donnybrook or worse.

Hawkes began yelling for Praeger to check first with the front office. Praeger paused and cupped his hand over the mouthpiece. "For Christ's sake, check with *who* in the front office? Gimpelman's on his way to the hospital. Winkle doesn't give a shit. Just who should I check with? *Old man Kane?*"

All the while a harsh female voice on the phone—with soul music blaring in the background—was assuring him that six officers would be dispatched immediately.

Dropping the phone, Praeger brushed Hawkes aside and entered the box office. Ida was still punching tickets. Teddy Winkle was sorting bills. "For Christ's sake!" said

Praeger. "Stop selling tickets, won't you! Don't you have any idea of the madhouse we have in there?"

Teddy Winkle waved him away. "We're selling standing room, selling standing room."

"You're insane."

"I know it, I know it!" He held out a fistful of banknotes. "We've got to keep selling tickets. The line's not going down. I've never seen anything like it. People aren't even waiting for change. . . ."

13

With his bank deposit bag locked and secure, the concession manager breathed easier.

"Uh, Mr. Lebowitz," said Praeger, "while we're having this little tête-à-tête, I think you should know the patrons are complaining about your extra tax again."

"What'd you mean by extra?"

"The couple cents you tell the girls to add on every sale."

"What are you talking? You a tax lawyer all of a sudden? *It's a service charge!*"

"A service charge for getting screwed?"

Lebowitz waved his hand. "Watch your step, Cliffie. Hiring you was Winkle's idea. Far as I'm concerned your background stinks. You know. So just stay out of my concession. It's none of your business."

"When people complain it's—"

"Can I help it if the tax charts get torn down?"

"I'll tattoo a chart on Cindy's wrist," said Praeger. "Just stop making her charge extra."

"What are you worried? I run things around here. I'm in charge of downtown."

Praeger sucked air through his teeth as he watched the

fat man scribble out a deposit slip. "Yeah. Until Winkle comes in."

"Winkle's an idiot."

No argument there, he thought. Stories enough circulated about Teddy Winkle to make Lebowitz appear saintly. It all started with The Great Winkle Water Fiasco, which occurred when Winkle first started in the business as the seventeen-year-old manager of the Belvedere. One night he had decided to hammer a peephole from the manager's office to the adjoining ladies' room. Chisel in hand, he was working on it after closing when he burst a water pipe, flooding the entire ground floor of the theatre. Before the water bureau emergency trucks arrived, before the gas and electric company cut the power in the area, before the street was cordoned off and spotlights set up, three feet of water accumulated at the base of the stage, submerging the front six rows in the orchestra.

"Look, Mr. Lebowitz," said Praeger. "All I want to do is keep the roof on and maybe leave at night with a clean conscience."

"*Clean conscience!* You want a clean conscience join the Salvation Army."

"I don't think you understand, Mr. Lebowitz."

"Understand what?"

"Me," said Praeger.

"I don't have to understand you, Cliffie baby. Your ass is on the way out. You been fraternizing with a cashier. Don't think I don't know. It's Michele from the Eagle. I ain't stupid. I see her come over here every night."

"Fraternizing? We're fucking living together."

Lebowitz's eyes widened.

"You interested? You want her? She's a bloody domestic disaster area. Toasted half the kitchen this morning."

"If she comes over here tonight, I'm going to report it."

The office buzzer sounded, signaling that a call was on hold. Praeger picked up the receiver and gave Lebowitz the finger at the same time.

Sidney Gimpelman, general manager and booker for Kane Theatres, was on the line. He wanted an okay put on the door for the following evening. An okay was parlance for a free admission.

"Send them down," said Praeger. "We can always use the body heat."

"When are the shows?"

"When can they get here?"

Gimpelman's end went silent for a moment. "Look, wise ass . . ."

"I've got a million of them," said Praeger, glancing up at Lebowitz hulking red-faced in the doorway.

"Motherfucker," the rotund man mumbled.

Praeger blew him a kiss and watched him stalk out, bank bag clutched to his breast.

"Goddamnit, Praeger!" squawked the tinny voice on the phone. "What are the show times?"

"Ten, twelve, two, four, six, eight, ten."

SUPERDUDE DAY

"Selling standing room, selling standing room," Teddy Winkle cackled.

Praeger stalked back to his office, slamming the box office door. His head was aswirl. He felt like taking the keys from his pocket, placing them neatly on the desk, and walking out.

He would, he knew, never make the sidewalk.

Hawkes was still there—entertaining similar ideas it seemed. "Fuck this," he said, looking at Praeger with disordered, jellyfish eyes. "Ain't no money in the world worth this bullshit. I'm going home." He unbolted the lobby door and opened it.

Immediately, a fist sprang through and popped him square in the nose.

He reeled backward, slapping his hand over a spurt of blood. Praeger lunged for the door and kept it from being flung wide, at the same time grabbing Hawkes and pulling him forward. "Help me, Goddamnit! Put some weight against it."

Together, kicking and pushing, they managed to secure the door. Once it was bolted, Hawkes promptly fell sobbing to the floor, holding his nose.

Praeger picked up the office phone and pressed the

69

local buzzer three times. Outside the door he could hear
pounding and screaming. "Ledbetter, listen to me," he
shouted. His breathing was erratic. "And don't say a
word. Not a whisper. You hear? I know for an absolute
fact you're hiding a print of *Mondo Sucko* up there."

"I ain't got—"

"Shup up a minute! I know you got it. And I know
how you got it, too, you thieving old man."

"But—"

"I know all about the after-hours parties at the censor
board offices, when they were showing it to friends. You
filled in as operator one night. Next day the print was
missing."

"Can't prove nothing."

"You're going to show it, you hear! I know it's the
filthiest piece of shit ever thrown together. I know not
even Gimpelman would show it. And I know we're both
going to jail if you show it. But *show it!* It's my responsibility. I'll take full responsibility. Now shut up, I told
you. I don't want to hear it. I don't give a fuck about
you or your union. Only one of two things can save this
place now—and that means you and me, too, Ledbetter
—either you go on stage in blackface and do the Superdude bit or put a ninety-minute blow job on screen. . . ."

Praeger's girl friend was named Michele Lithe. She was from Brooklyn and was spending her second year at Godward, tuition courtesy stepfather. She picked up spending money by working five nights a week at Kane's Eagle Theatre. She further hedged on expenses by living with Clifton Praeger.

"Poor Praeger," she would say, "everybody's got a cross to bear—but you've got a Star of David."

Each evening, after the Eagle box office closed, she would troop the five blocks to Stricker Street. . . .

16

SUPERDUDE DAY

The pandemonium subsided when *Mondo Sucko* went on. Everyone had heard of it—yet few had actually seen it. A *cause célèbre* in a dozen courts about the country, its absolute obscenity and utter lack of redeeming social value was unquestioned, even by the defense. The national news magazines had featured its star, Vita Vibes, on their covers. Without doubt, it was one gross hunk of film, admitted even Vita in interview.

Chants for Superdude all but vanished.

The audience settled into a state of wide-eyed disbelief as Vita Vibes took a ten-incher, black as licorice, into her mouth, then a yellow into her vagina, and a white into her anus—the latter two a bit less foreboding than the first.

Heavy stuff, very symbolic.

Praeger was finally able to leave the office. He made his way—all the while listening to complaints from parent-patrons and patron-prudes—to the vestibule ticket stand to see if Brother Jason was still among the breathing.

He was.

17

Michele Lithe was raped in the Rococo balcony that winter night.

On the threadbare carpet between rows FF and GG to be precise, with Ledbetter in the booth above seeing nothing, with the police in the auditorium below hearing nothing.

Praeger found her in the side alley, beneath the ramp leading from a pried-open exit door. She was laying among broken wine bottles and piles of hobo dung. She was semiconscious. Something had been smashed across her head.

Dozens of cars came, with blue flashing lights, with swaggering men in blue coats. Then an ambulance came to take her away. Its light was red. Cursing and struggling, Praeger attempted to go along, but the police restrained him.

"Did you know her?" he was asked.

"Yes. Yes, of course. She's cashier at the Eagle. She's my girl friend. . . ."

"She come to see you or the movie?"

"Me."

"When did you last see her?"

"In the office. I had some phone calls to make. She went in to watch the movie until I was through."

"You let her go alone?"

"There were four old ladies and three fucking police in there. I thought she might be safe."

"Okay, okay. So nobody else bought a ticket? Just the ladies? That right?"

"Yes."

"You notice anybody strange hanging around the theatre tonight?"

"Besides the cops?"

"Look, friend, we want to nail this cocksucker. . . ."

"All right. Yeah. There was some clown wandering around outside before the last show. Had like this Swedish army coat with fur pelts hanging off it and these purple knee-high boots."

"A nigger?"

"A black person," said Praeger.

"What did he look like?"

"He looked like shit."

"*Christ*—I mean physical description . . . you know."

"Tall. Skinny. Early twenties. Mustache."

"He come inside?"

"No."

"You talk to him at all?"

"No."

"Would you recognize him again?"

Praeger shrugged.

A K-9 man approached with his dog held tight against his left leg. His name was Stuart. Praeger knew him. They got off work at the same hour some nights and would stop for a beer.

Stuart was among those who had been cat-napping in the auditorium.

"Cliff, I'm sorry," he said, "but none of us heard a thing."

Tell it to the girl, Praeger felt like saying, but he didn't. The whole scene was beginning to smack of Friday night TV—especially the dialogue. *Tell it to the girl,* was definitely his next line, uttered with rightful indignation. *Jesus, Jesus, tell me something! Like tell me none of this is happening.*

"Didn't hear a thing," Stuart repeated.

Praeger went berserk, crying: "All of you get out! I don't want no asshole police in this theatre. Not as long as I'm manager, you hear? All of you hear? And tell them downtown . . . tell them in the saloons tonight . . . tell them any bloody fucking place you want to—but I don't want any of you bastards near the Rococo. Never again. . . ." He then began swinging.

After Praeger was taken outside and handcuffed to a parking meter to cool off, the quartet of ladies being detained for questioning finally spoke up. They described how, before the intermission, a tall black boy had chased a girl down the right aisle, across the front of the screen, then up the left aisle.

"I didn't think darkies were allowed in these places," one said.

SUPERDUDE DAY

As the guards arrived—unintelligible dark princes, swaggering, clad in jackboots, leather jackets, black Nazi-type hats, quick-draw holsters slung low on the hip—Praeger assigned them, placing a pair to help Brother Jason tear tickets and bar crashers, one to the lobby, another brace to the auditorium, and one to patrol the Grand Staircase and balcony.

The effect was immediate. Movement within the innards of the Rococo appeared suddenly under control—not actual in-good-conscience control, but at least an aura. *Mondo Sucko* showed to a quiet audience. Some patrons, disgusted with Vita Vibes, gave up their seats and left the theatre. Others crowded in. Praeger could feel spurts of hope flowing through his veins. He had more than an hour to get Superdude on stage.

All at once it was a challenge: keeping everything cocordinated, making it work, repressing calamity and disaster as they fell like dominoes. The entire fiasco had —piece and bit at a time—been dropped on him and he meant to pull it off.

One way or another.

Stopping in the vestibule, he instructed Brother Jason and the two rent-a-cops to announce "standing room only" before accepting tickets. If Teddy Winkle wanted standing room only, standing room only it would be.

Now, free to maneuver, he made his way to the rear of the lobby. Complaints of smoke were being yelled into his ear. Someone had dropped a lit cigarette into a vent. Decades of dusty debris were smoldering. He stopped the fans, removed the vent guard, and emptied a fire extinguisher into the duct. After a brief wait he restarted the fans. Steam, rancid and ocher, poured from the vent. But no smoke.

Other patrons, with wet feet, began describing a flood, pointing upstairs.

An inch of water covered the floor of the men's lavatory off the upper concourse. Praeger waded in. A urinal was overflowing, running incessantly; the drains were clogged with hot dog wrappers, bits of food, discarded towels.

He found a screwdriver in the supply closet and cut the water.

Men and boys continued to crowd in, walking duck-like, using the urinals; their waste found no drain—instead, it dissipated in the flood. Soon, a dappled reeking sea remained, lapping the walls, its wake escaping the open doorway, seeping under the carpeting, flowing down the steps.

A tube was stuck up Michele's nose. Her head, covered with sterile bandage, resembled a globe—with one eye and a portion of cheek the only topography. "Some fucking theatre you run," she mumbled.

She was in intensive care.

"Baby, I'm sorry," said Praeger. "Really, you don't know. . . ."

"How'd you get in?"

"Walked in."

"Well, why don't you just walk out."

His stare dwelled on what little of her was free of bandage or bedclothes: the sallow skin puffed about a demiface, reminding him of an overripe body he had once seen in Nam.

"How's the kitten?" she asked.

"*What* kitten?"

"The stray calico I took in last week. Goddamnit, Praeger, you better be feeding my animals. How's Ralph?"

"Ralph's fine—except she went into heat."

"How's Gomer?"

"Gomer's just great. He shit on the rug again."

"Oh, that bad Gomer. Wait till I get home. Just wait. Did the vet call about the beagle yet?"

"Yeah," said Praeger. "He wanted to put it to sleep."

She struggled to sit up. "I'll put that shithead to sleep! What happened? Did you pick her up?"

"Yes, of course I picked her up. What do you think? I even visited Baldy."

"*Oh, my God!* Poor Baldy. I haven't paid in two weeks—"

"I took care of it. Look, the whole bloody menagerie's just fine. Including Baldy. Don't worry about them."

"I worry."

"Yes, I know." Praeger entwined his hand with hers. "I love you, baby," he whispered. "I do love you."

"Ditto," said Michele.

Praeger was quiet for a moment. "That black guy do it?" he asked at last. "The one dressed up like Tarzan of the Apes."

"Yeah, that's him," she said, then paused before adding: "It was strange, Praeger, really strange."

"What do you mean?"

"He had the ugliest, most grotesque look on his face . . . like he wasn't enjoying what he was doing at all." She rocked her head side to side. "It's all right though."

"What?"

"Told me he'd marry me . . . told me all kind of crap . . . called me his hot honky pudding when he got me outside. *Shit.* I'm glad something was hot in that alley. . . ."

Praeger said nothing. He merely looked at her.

"Shit," she repeated, almost an echo.

"What happened to your head?"

"He cold-cocked me. With a brick. I had hold of that weirdo, too. Right by the gonads."

Again, Praeger said nothing.

"Don't worry," she muttered. "The fascista'll pick him up. Then I'm going to get *his* pudding for breach of promise."

"Huh?"

"I told you, dumb-dumb, he promised to marry me. . . ."

Suddenly, Praeger's arms fell limp. A flush of helplessness caused him to slide into the chair at bedside. "Jesus Christ, Michele," he said quietly.

A middle-aged nurse in starched whites entered the room. She stopped short, leering at Praeger. "How'd you get in?"

"Walked in."

"You from the police?"

"A friend."

"Some bloody friend . . ." chortled Michele.

"You'll have to leave," said the nurse. "This is a restricted area."

Praeger nodded. Before getting up he leaned forward and kissed Michele's bandage.

"Don't! Don't do that!" yelled the nurse, grabbing him by the elbow. "Infection! Infection!" In the commotion a water pitcher tumbled from the bed table. Praeger got down on his hands and knees trying to retrieve the thing as it rolled under the bed.

"Look, Wonder Woman," said Michele. "He wants to kiss me, let him kiss me."

The nurse, for some reason, lapsed into baby talk. "You wantsum to get well, don't you, whittle girl?"

Michele looked at her incredulously. "Why don't you go suture an asshole," she said.

Taken aback, the nurse stammered, "That's . . . that's quite enough from you, young lady."

"*Jesus*, Michele," said Praeger, looking up from the floor, "save a few one-liners for the mortician."

"Don't *Jesus* me, Praeger. I'm Jewish."

The nurse glared at them. "All right. You two want to play games. All right. We'll play games." She turned on her toes, leaving to call the head nurse, two orderlies, and a security guard.

Teddy Winkle was at the Rococo when Praeger walked in, sitting at Praeger's desk among scattered papers, pizza crusts, and empty coffee cups, resting his head in a web of fingers.

"God, Cliff, I'm glad you're here. It's unreal. I'm going out of my mind. Gimpelman's on his way over. Something super brewing." Suddenly he became secretive, half-whispering. "And Hawkes didn't show today. His own mother hasn't even seen him."

Praeger shrugged, belching the Scotch he had downed before coming in. "It's Christmas party week. He'll show eventually. Don't worry."

At times Praeger felt almost paternal about Teddy Winkle. He was *so* helpless. Praeger remembered two months back, to Halloween night, when a group of black street thugs (nary a one in costume) had come to the doorman's station demanding to see the manager. Teddy Winkle had been in the office at the time; Praeger was out getting the evening papers.

"Trick or treat," the gang's leader said.

"Stricker Street?" echoed Teddy Winkle, dumbfounded, thinking they were asking directions. "This *is* Stricker Street."

"No, man, trick or treat."

"Stricker Street?" repeated Teddy Winkle, pitying the poor boy his speech impediment.

"Trick or treat, motherfucker!"

Praeger returned just in time to prevent Teddy Winkle from being squashed into the lobby carpet. He put on his Bogart act and shooed the boys away, then he had to explain to Teddy Winkle that they were merely trying to trick-or-treat their way into the movies.

"Oh . . ." was all Teddy Winkle could say.

Praeger looked at him now, smiling as he recalled the incident. "Relax. Everything'll work out."

"God, I hope so. I'm going out of my mind. Cashier didn't show at the Granada. *Nobody* showed at the Belvedere. I'm going out of my mind. Bad publicity's killing us here. The check machine's gonna have a coronary for sure. My God, and I owe every bookie on the Strip. They're gonna cut my balls off. They're gonna make me cement overshoes. They're gonna dump my ass in the harbor. . . ." He paused, opening his suit coat, unbuttoning his shirt. "Unless, unless," he yelled, jumping up, dancing about the office, "they see *this!*"

He was wearing his blue and red Superman T-shirt.

Mr. Gimpelman walked in. "What the fuck are you doing?"

Gimpelman hated Teddy Winkle. Teddy Winkle represented nepotism. Nepotism represented a threat to Gimpelman's good standing. Gimpelman hated all threats to his good standing. He was a man enclosed in an impregnable cyclone of motion. Old man Kane liked motion. Of course, Teddy Winkle possessed his own ambulant cyclone—more flung than enclosed by it, but the results were often spectacular.

To avoid being walked over, Praeger moved out of Gimpelman's way.

Everyone, to Praeger's mind, looked like somebody in the movies, and Gimpelman—a bit over five feet tall with bushy eyebrows and a gruff voice—definitely resembled Yosemite Sam from Loony Tunes. The semblance was uncanny. Praeger was forever waiting for him to say, "*All right, where's that varmit wabbit!*"

Gimpelman had no use for Praeger either.

"All right, here's what we're going to do," said Gimpelman. "For two days now no business. Right. Not even freebies. Not even sneak-ins. Not even police—"

"Three days," said Teddy Winkle.

"Shut up, huh. I've got oyster-roast tickets in my pocket I'd like to use sometime today. You think I like coming in on Sunday? I want to get this over with, okay?"

"Right," said Teddy Winkle, buttoning his shirt.

"We haven't had a carbon lit here since you-know-who got fucked in the balcony. TV crews sit outside all day filming the marquee. Anybody fool enough to buy a ticket gets interviewed for the six o'clock news." He flicked cigar ashes in the direction of Praeger's desk. "Christmas holidays are supposed to be blockbusters. Heavy grosses. And we're going to die—flat-out die. I've called Washington. I'm dumping this hunk of shit. Fuck Julie Andrews *and* the distributor. Papers are screaming rape. Everybody in the city thinks Rococo they think rape. Rape. Rape. Rape. Right?"

"Right," said Teddy Winkle.

"Well, you know what? *We're going to give them rape.* Starting Christmas Day we're going with sexploitation."

"Great, great," said Teddy Winkle.

Gimpelman looked up at Praeger. "I'll get the schedules and shit to you. Get the marquee and recording changed Christmas Eve, be sure the prints are in, change your displays, and put up X-rating cards. I don't want any stupid fuckups."

Stupide, stupide.

"And the censor board?" asked Praeger. *Christ,* he thought, *when The Umbrella Lady sees this she'll flush head-first down a commode—without her life jacket.*

"Screw them. I'm going to take a chance."

"What about me?" said Teddy Winkle.

But Gimpelman was gone.

Praeger picked up a trash can and walked about the office shoveling the day's residue into it. "I'll check out the matinee girl. Why don't you take off. I can handle things here."

"Yeah, yeah," said Teddy Winkle, groping to regain some sprig of authority. "I've got to make it to the Eagle. Benny's been filling in as manager."

"Give him my love."

Winkle twisted his head sideward. "He's all right. Just like Gimpelman. You just got to understand him, that's all. Just got to understand him."

"I understand him."

At that instant Benny Lebowitz's bulk plugged the doorframe. "What'd Gimpelman want?"

"What are you doing *here!*" Teddy Winkle slumped back into Praeger's chair, holding his forehead. "Holy hell. Who's at the Eagle? I can't stand it. I can't stand it. You can't be here."

"It's five o'clock," said Lebowitz. "That drunk of a

night manager showed and I left. You know, I got my own business to run. You ever think of that? Who's been watching my stands all day?"

"Why's everything always happen to me?" said Teddy Winkle, his head dropping to the desk.

"What'd Gimpelman want?"

Suddenly, gleefully, Teddy Winkle looked up. "We're gonna be a porno palace!"

SUPERDUDE DAY

A trio of obese black women in nurse's garb cornered Praeger as he sloshed toward the balcony. They wanted their money back. Superdude was supposed to be there in the flesh, they complained. They wanted to see Superdude, not some jive skin flick.

They also complained about getting wet feet.

Praeger led them to Winkle's office and unlocked the door. "There he is, ladies." They looked at Praeger questioningly for an instant—only an instant—then plummeted in.

Superdude was still crouched in the corner with the cape over his head. The nurses rushed to him, cackling and cooing.

"My man!" came a plea from the corner as Praeger walked out. "*My man!*"

Dozens of people brushed past him as he secured and locked the door. They all seemed to be complaining, quite adamantly complaining, in whispers, yells, and screams.

His scouting of the balcony for empty seats would have to wait. Too much to be done elsewhere. Elsewhere and *everywhere!* Things were slipping out of control again. Rapidly, he was becoming enraged that it all was being left to him—to keep things together, to get Superdude on stage, to give the people the show Kane Theatres had advertised—as if he, Clifton Praeger, were personally responsible. . . .

Reaching the base of the Grand Staircase, a woman in leopard-skin leotards approached asking if the ladies' room could be cleaned: someone had defecated into a washbowl.

He assured her he would see about it.

Brother Jason came back long enough to tell him that All-Star security guards were selling people through the front door without tickets, dollar a head. Praeger grunted and thanked him.

He turned in time to stop two youngsters from demolishing the soda machine. For a quarter, ice and soda would slosh down—sans cup. He folded a matchbook and jammed it into the coin slot.

Immediately, from nowhere, a hulking All-Star collared him from behind. Praeger twisted away and calmly explained that he was the manager, *remember*.

I am, my God, I am the manager, he thought. *I am the one who's responsible. . . .*

GIANT HOLIDAY SEXSATION SHOW
HOT SPUR
and
LOVE THY NEIGHBOR . . .
AND HIS WIFE

Christmas morning Praeger had breakfast at a White Tower. Two hamburgers and coffee. Then he went downtown. With Hawkes still among the missing he had been working double shifts, open to close.

Another of Dewey's notes awaited him. Funny happenings were continuing backstage. Praeger read it and filed it. Dewey, he realized, was becoming a pain in the ass.

Business started slow. After The Umbrella Lady and The Button Man had found their separate seats, a half-dozen corseted and corsaged ladies appeared, thinking the Julie Andrews extravaganza was still playing. Praeger tried to discourage them but they insisted on buying tickets.

They came out ten minutes later wanting refunds.

After dinner it started to pick up, in dribbles at first, then—as word of mouth filtered down to the bus station and transient hotels and cafeterias—the downtown crazies began to appear: Sergeant Major Sam, Maggie the whore, Lippo from the Greyhound baggage room, Alonzo the punchy ex-middleweight, Stickman, Cowboy John—many others too, others that Praeger knew only by sight, including half the bums from the Mission House. Praeger, in proper holiday spirit, passed most through without benefit of ticket.

Later in the evening, couples began to arrive, and groups of bleary-eyed servicemen up from the Strip, and solitary gentlemen with overcoats.

It seemed Gimpelman knew what he was doing.

The night before, as Harry Harp, Praeger's one-armed, lame-of-leg, fifty-year-old usher changed the marquee in accordance with copy supplied by the front office, Praeger had stayed outside helping him hang letters, all the while tempted to have the man put up a different version, at least for a time:

GIANT HOLIDAY SEXSATION SHOW
JESUS CHRIST MEETS LOLITA
and
SANTA CLAUS GETS LAID

He was glad he hadn't.

Gimpelman had stopped his Coupe DeVille in the middle of Stricker Street just as they were lowering the ladder. He was dressed in dinner clothes and his wife was beside him, in mink. The electric window hummed down long enough for him to say, "They want shit, we'll give them shit! They want fuck-fuck kill-kill, we'll give them fuck-fuck kill-kill."

The electric window hummed up and he drove away.

The hangover stretch between Christmas and New Year's was a delight to the accounting office of Kane Theatres. Each day, Praeger and his coworkers would assemble to find warm bodies awaiting the unlocking of doors—actual money-in-hand customers. By show time hundreds of them would be seated and settled. *Hot Spur* went on screen first. A sweaty silence would befall the auditorium as skin and pubic hair started to flash.

Sheltered by fifty prudish years of municipal censoring, the locals were ill-prepared for *Hot Spur*.

Yet none complained.

Glued cloth to seat, they were enthralled with Gimpelman's unexpurgated holiday offering: a Chicano raping and torturing—to the accompaniment of fandango rhythms —the wife of a peanut farmer.

Hawkes showed the second day of the New Year with some outlandish story about being abducted to a commune farmhouse in the boondocks by two nymphomaniacs in a red Volkswagen. He had just managed to escape that morning and had hitched straight back to the city and, of course, work. Praeger called it wishful thinking, but Teddy Winkle believed every word—in fact, became angry because Hawkes hadn't called him when he met the pair. Two minutes later, though, he lost interest upon learning one was a redhead and the other a brunette.

Teddy Winkle associated only with blondes. *Naturel.*

Now that Hawkes was safely back, Praeger took a few days off. Spending afternoons visiting Michele and evenings pie-eyed in the pubs of Guinness Village, he missed the uproar caused by the Municipal Board of Censors.

With the holidays, with city offices closed, Gimpelman had been certain he could sneak by with an uncensored film for a week or two. He had done it before. Whet the appetite of the public, fatten up the accounts, then go back to playing it legit.

It was a simple, even basic, business practice. How was he to know everything would turn to shit?

The Municipal Board of Censors was in big trouble. They were about to become extinct. The city council was eyeing their budget in closed session.

No budget. No board.

They were a triumvirate, politically appointed. The position was part-time. They liked the hours, the salary, and the prestige. They were determined not to lose their budget. They had to think of something—quick.

By law every film entering the city was supposed to be viewed by the board and either given a seal of approval or rejected. Since the three members were rarely at their office-screening room, the assigned projectionist usually ended up running a footage count on the prints as they came in, sticking a seal in the can, and stacking them for pickup.

The assigned projectionist was the single most powerful man in local cinema circles.

In justness, the board did find time to view two types of films: highly touted productions with top stars and anything containing so much as a wrinkle of sex. They weren't allowed to scissor what "offended" them in the latter—but they could *suggest* cuts. Most distributors complied and resubmitted.

Theatres around the city, as a result of their handiwork, showed some of the most chopped-up aberrations conceivable.

If challenged in court, the board had a jack-in-the-box consultant ready to take the stand to define and present their views. Their views often changed with the weather, menstrual cycles, and the daily horoscope in the *News Record*.

Their qualifications to be determining what could or couldn't be viewed by millions of the citizenry was a standing joke among millions of the citizenry. Of the reigning triad, known locally as The Three Stooges, only one had been to college—a pharmacist who had contributed heavily to the mayor's last campaign. The remaining two, both ladies, were something less than alike. One was the blowzy, foul-mouthed wife of a ward politico; the other was a bleeding-heart puritan who envisaged this subjection to dirty movies as some personal cross designed by God to atone for the sins of the world. The latter was loony and largely left alone by her coworkers.

In their scramble for survival the board began going over newspaper listings, inspecting theatres, scouring their files for that something, that anything. Quite by chance they stumbled upon *Hot Spur* at the Rococo and, elated, immediately went behind locked doors to join heads.

Next morning their spokesperson approached the media with an astonishing story: the showing of an uncensored sex film at the Rococo Theatre had caused that poor coed to be raped before Christmas.

For two days they rode high. They had found their *something*. Then a reporter reminded them that a Julie Andrews movie was playing at the time of the attack. The faux pas mattered little. Parents enough had been terrified into thinking that their daughters would be molested in theatre aisles no matter what the film—so long as it lacked the seal of the Municipal Board of Censors. By week's end the city council approved the board's budget for another twelvemonth, and the municipal court gave Gimpelman a fat fine.

Never again, the board promised the mayor (who had two daughters of his own), would such filth plague the city's screens.

SUPERDUDE DAY

Wading his way through catastrophe and complaint, Praeger reached the vestibule and let himself into the box office. Hawkes was sitting on a chair holding his swollen face. Teddy Winkle stood next to the auxiliary box office window, sweating profusely, hovering over Ida like a fiend from Transylvania. "I love it, I love it," he was mumbling. His shirt and suit coat were soaked—and the purple lettering on the Superdude T-shirt he wore over them was beginning to run.

"Superdude refused to go on stage," said Praeger quietly, deliberately, as if presenting a rehearsed report. "So I'm showing *Mondo Sucko* instead."

Duty done, he turned to leave.

Teddy Winkle seemed oblivious of everything except the money passing through the window slot. He gave Praeger a blank look, for only an instant, before grabbing his arm. "Cliff, Cliff, where've you been?" he cried. "Go down the bank and get more quarters. Get a thousand in quarters." He scooped up a bundle of money and thrust it at him.

"Banks are closed," said Praeger.

"*Closed?*"

"It's a holiday." Turning away, he opened the door to

94

the adjoining office. He went directly to the safe, knelt down, and began spinning the dial.

Teddy Winkle followed him, hopping like a rabbit. "You know, you're right! What're we going to do? I can't sell tickets without quarters. . . ."

Praeger's fingers worked rhythmically over the numerals.

"What are we going to do?"

"I don't know about you," Praeger said simply as he pulled open the lead door and extracted a .44 magnum revolver, "but I'm going to talk Superdude into going on stage."

"Cliff! *Jesus* . . ."

Praeger raised the revolver. "And you're going to stop selling tickets."

"All right, Cliff, look, just look," said Teddy Winkle in a quaver of a voice. "Just put the gun back and listen, huh? Just listen and be reasonable, huh. I know you're upset. But we can't stop selling. It's unreal, Cliff. They just keep coming. It's unreal. Superdude or no Superdude. We can't stop selling."

Praeger opened the chamber of the revolver with a flip of the hand. Teddy Winkle was impressed. He had never seen it done better, even in the movies.

"Well," Teddy Winkle said, slowly. "I guess we could stop for a while. After all, we do need quarters."

Praeger closed the chamber of the revolver with another flip.

Teddy Winkle surveyed him. He had never seen Praeger enraged, had never before noticed the insane cast about his eyes. "In fact, I'm pretty sure we could stop for a while—least till we get quarters."

Praeger tucked the revolver out of sight and entered the lobby. With him gone, Teddy Winkle told Ida to keep selling tickets, *keep selling tickets,* but to tell the people they couldn't go in. He then sat down and began some serious worrying about quarters.

Worrying about Praeger would have to wait.

Teddy Winkle found a solution.

He sent Hawkes on a pilgrimage after The Button Man. The Button Man always had pockets full of quarters. The Button Man was as good as a bank when it came to quarters.

Hawkes sprang at the opportunity. He was grateful to be away from the theatre. Even if things had quieted. The sight of Praeger running around with that cannon had unnerved him.

Praeger stalked through the lobby, stopping face to face with the security guard stationed in the front vestibule. "Nobody else comes in until I say so. And keep this bank of doors closed. Anybody wants to go out, fine. But nobody comes in."

The guard grunted.

"And one other thing," said Praeger. "You want to make money in the movie business—build a theatre of your own and stop ripping us off."

The guard rolled his eyes.

With the help of Brother Jason and a second All-Star they managed to secure the front. A few people who'd already been in got shuffled outside in the confusion. They tried to fight their way back in, pounding the doors, faces pressed like leaves against the glass. The crowd behind continued swaying, pushing forward, flattening them. Angrily, a woman spit at Praeger—as if her saliva would penetrate the glazed surface; another waved a torn stub, pleading through the glass that she'd only gone to get popcorn for her children. Another had left her seat for a smoke. Others joined with their own complaints as they ranted and kicked at the doorframes, calling him the same tired old names.

He went back to the office and quickly lettered a sign on cardboard, then returned and taped it to the glass, facing outward.

ONLY HOMOSEXUALS WILL BE ADMITTED
UNTIL THE FIRST SHOW ENDS
ALL OTHERS PLEASE FORM A LINE

Five minutes later, an All-Star approached Praeger in the lobby. "What the fuck's wrong with those jiveasses out there?"

"Huh?"

"Look," he said, motioning him toward the street. "I never see'd nothin' like *this*."

Outside, among the littered remains of Superdude's pimpmobile, the street was filled with people playing queer. Dozens of them swishing up and down the sidewalk. Sashaying boys kissing other boys, making prissy hand gestures. Women laughing hysterically. Hugging one another. One toothsome girl on her knees, lapping at the dress of another. Each trying to outdo the other.

The security guard fingered his holstered firearm. "I

never see'd nothin' like this," he repeated. "Even when I was doing time."

Hawkes found The Button Man sleeping at a table in Bickford's. He shook him awake and led him back to the theatre, explaining that he had been chosen as guest of honor for the day.

The Button Man grinned.

All they asked, Hawkes added, was for him to sell the box office some quarters.

The Button Man grunted and, without looking, tapped a button on his left sleeve.

Kiss Me You Fool, it said.

Early the first Monday of the New Year, Praeger went by Union General to pick up Michele. Condition improved, she had been moved into a semiprivate room. Otherwise, Praeger soon discovered, all was not going well. Stepping from the elevator he was met with sounds of an argument. Michele's voice was recognizable. She was bandying the word *Gestapo* in full pitch.

"You here to get her?" asked the desk nurse; she looked rather haggard, which struck Praeger as unusual since the shifts had just changed. The woman exhaled an audible sigh when Praeger nodded. She rose and pointed him toward the commotion.

Michele was pacing about the room in bedclothes. "Goddamn the rules! She was in pain. She was suffering." An intern and a black nurse were trying to calm her. The corner bed held a shriveled Italian woman, glowing with the attention she was getting, yet, at the same time, shaking her head and hedging, "No trouble, no trouble . . ."

Praeger paused in the doorway.

"Trouble? These Mickey Mouse sadists would let you croak for a hand of gin rummy. Sitting out there all night, joking and giggling, drinking Pepsi-Cola while people suffer and *die*! It's perverse."

"Look," said the nurse, "we just came on duty."

"That's it! Shift the weight. Just like a good Nazi."

The intern held up a clipboard. "Her chart says that something was administered at one A.M."

"*Something*, what's something?" cried Michele. "Sugar pills?" She caught a glimpse of Praeger in the doorway. "Goddamnit, Praeger, come here and punch this little turd in the nose."

"Get dressed, baby. Time to go. The animal kingdom needs you."

Fifty-three minutes later—suitcase, flowers, cards, and candy in arm—he managed to steer her from the room. She still wasn't dressed, although she had agreed to a bathrobe. As he led her past the nurse's station she was screaming, "You fascists, next time I get raped see if I come back here!"

"Who's taking the chains off the exits?"

"I do it every day," said Praeger, dumping an ashtray into his office trash can.

"Those doors got to stay chained," Lebowitz said. He looked at Teddy Winkle. The pair had just come down from their hideaway en route to dinner. "I say they stay chained. If the doors were chained little girls wouldn't get themselves raped."

"Let me worry about it," said Praeger.

"You're asking for trouble with exit doors unlocked, Cliffie. Those street niggers sneak in and rob my stand blind. Got to keep the little bastards out. I won't have niggers getting near my food. You know what I mean? Doors got to stay chained." He turned to Teddy Winkle. "Either that or bring in security guards."

"Oh, God!" said Teddy Winkle. "The check machine would have pulmonary emphysema."

"So what's the problem?" bellowed Lebowitz. "Chains are cheaper than guards!"

As usual, Teddy Winkle wavered. "All right, okay," he said. "Leave them chained, Cliff. Okay?"

"What about the fire inspector?"

Lebowitz slackened his tone. "He's been sitting his dead ass around all day watching skin flicks. Shame on him if he reports anything. Right, Cliffie baby? Right? You've seen him."

Praeger said nothing. It wasn't worth arguing. Lebowitz just naturally thought everybody was of his own mold: lazy and corruptible. The fire inspectors of the city were uniformly honest, dedicated, and conscientious; Lebowitz had them mixed up with the building inspectors, the housing code inspectors, the water and sewer inspectors, the health department inspectors, the electrical inspectors. . . .

Teddy Winkle shuffled a handful of papers together and pulled his overcoat from the rack; Lebowitz, all the while, hovered in the doorway with a smirk on his face, practicing deep breathing.

"I'll be over the Belvedere," Teddy Winkle said to Praeger, "but if anybody calls tell them I'm at the Eagle."

"Yeah, I'll go with you, Ted," said Lebowitz. "Where you want to eat? Dinner's on me."

"Oyster Bay'll be all right," said Teddy Winkle.

Praeger banged his fist into the file cabinet. When the hurt went away he walked out into the lobby.

"Boss man," came a voice from behind, "Mr. Winkle had me locks up the exit doors."

It was Brother Jason.

"And that man Mr. Lebowitz told me to clean his stock room and box popcorn."

"Let his help do it," said Praeger.

"He done fired his stock boy. I heard him saying so to Mr. Winkle."

"Fired him?"

"Yeah. Ain't that something? He won't pay no boy when he says I can do it all. He said if you wants to hire black peoples then lets the black peoples do the work. Told Mr. Winkle that. Mr. Winkle didn't say anything."

"Mr. Winkle likes fancy restaurants."

"Huh?"

Praeger reached back inside the office and plucked the exit keys from above the pay phone. "You just stick to your job," he said, on his way to unlock the doors the old man had just chained. "I'll have a talk with Mr. Lebowitz."

"Okay, boss."

Winkle and Lebowitz, he mumbled to himself, starting up the Grand Staircase. *Christ! Chaining exits in theatres!* Again, he was beginning to have doubts about the saneness of working with these people—the teen-age sex fiend and his faithful check-picker-upper, El Rotundo. *Worse than Laurel and Hardy.*

After unlocking the balcony exits, Praeger walked to the uppermost landing, then climbed the ladder to the projection booth, flashing his light. The auditorium exits would have to wait.

Waldo Ledbetter, the projectionist, was due a thera-
peutic visit.

An elfin man in baggy shorts and T-shirt, Ledbetter
shot a terror-struck look at the entranceway. Funny papers slid in a heap to the floor. Then, seeing it was
Praeger, he relaxed and exhaled a chesty breath.

"Holy hell, Cliff," he shouted above the roar of ancient
machinery, "I thought it was the mad rapist come to get
me."

"No, only me."

"Can't be too careful around here. Operator got held
up out at the drive-in last week. I'd bolt the door shut, except it gets hot as a furnace." He stood to pick up the
funnies. "Hey, when you going to order some decent carbons—these things here come from Hong Kong. I've been
going off screen two three times a night."

"I'll send them up with your Christmas bonus."

Ledbetter roared, jumping about like a leprechaun,
slapping his side. Finally he settled down and wiped tears
from his cheeks. "Really," he said, "these things are
nothing but crap. Plain crap. Had two positives crumble
already today."

"I'll memo the office."

"Appreciate that, boss."

"Everything else all right?"

"Right as rain."

As Praeger started back down, Ledbetter called after
him, asking to have an usher deliver coffee. "Those other
bastards let a guy rot." The voice followed Praeger as he
descended the ladder. "Last one didn't even know where
the booth was. Thought the prints got on screen by
magic, I guess. Had to call the union on his ass, the son-

ofabitch. Never got goodies sent up or nothing. You know, some of them jokers think it's easy sitting in this hole for fourteen hours. Well I'll tell you something, it ain't. Enough to drive you crazy up here. Hey, where you going? Stay and talk awhile."

"I'm due downstairs, Waldo."

"Wait! Wait! There's something else I forgot. I've been wanting to tell you. It's weird. I've been seeing shadows behind the screen some days—like somebody moving around. Especially on dark shots. And during afternoons too, when there's backlight. Definitely somebody back there. Who you think it is? Think it's those bums you let in? Or maybe it's the nigger what raped the girl. . . ."

Praeger went down into the balcony where he could hear no more.

Moving along the loge, on his way to unchain the remaining exits, he glanced over the railing. Below, in the orchestra, a portly man sitting close to the screen, overcoat spread open, trousers down about his ankles, was masturbating into one of Benny Lebowitz's hot dog rolls.

Sensing someone watching, the man looked around the empty rows, then, finally, upward at Praeger. Libido obviously outweighing any bent toward social conscience, he slouched down in the seat and hurriedly finished himself off while ogling a young thing on screen in panties and bra. He then slid the impregnated roll under the seat, buttoned up, and fled for a side exit.

Unfortunately, it was chained.

SUPERDUDE DAY

With *Mondo Sucko* still showing, with the front secure, with All-Star rent-a-cops in evidence, Praeger found himself staggering about the lobby, head spinning, knowing a myriad of disasters awaited—yet, without the vaguest notion of where to start.

A fat crab of a hand grabbed him from behind. "You got to help me, Cliffie. Just this once. We can't handle it."

Praeger stared at the arm holding him.

"Just help out for ten or twenty minutes," the voice pleaded. "I've got to get stuff from the storeroom. All I'm asking is ten minutes."

"Forget it."

"Come on, Cliffie baby, just this once."

Praeger pulled his shoulder free. "Stay away from me, Lebowitz."

"Just this one time."

A huge woman toting three kids jostled past Praeger, knocking him into a man in a bus driver's uniform, who, in turn, looked as if he wanted to punch Praeger in the mouth. Someone else started yelling at him about filthy this and filthy that in the ladies' room. Another with sopping pant legs complained about the men's room. Praeger

105

raised his arms, motioning that he would take care of it.

"What about my stand?" Lebowitz shouted above the din. "I'm losing business! Thieving brats are sneaking in the exits. You don't know what's going on—"

"Go fuck a duck."

"What'd you say?"

"Look, Lebowitz," said Praeger, extracting the .44 magnum revolver from under his coat, "I intend on getting Superdude's ass on stage. You know what I mean?"

Lebowitz's mouth fell open.

"And if anybody interferes," he said, waving the revolver, "I'll blow 'em away."

25

Business at the Rococo dropped off after the holidays. Business, it seemed, was disastrous everywhere. Editorials proclaimed it to be a combination of inflation during recession; others said recession during inflation. Labor blamed Management. Management blamed Government. Government blamed Labor and Management.

Gimpelman continued booking sexploitation films—although censored—into the Rococo, his thinking being, recession-inflation or not, the spread thighs of a voluptuous blonde was, historically, a commodity of no small interest to Labor, Management, or Government, or any other claque of voyeurs with three bucks.

Praeger would open the theatre on those days when Hawkes was off or among the missing. Loitering about the sidewalk, he would find a dozen middle-aged men, faces entombed in newspapers—the goons, as he called them. All innocently awaiting buses.

When Ida Schmidt pulled her cashier's curtain, they would sidle up to the box office one by one as if part of an invisible queue, pluck down exact admission, and disappear past the doorman without waiting for a stub. Once in the auditorium they would scatter. Canon of conduct

107

was observed. Six rows separated each of them. And each was equipped with a newspaper or overcoat for his lap.

During matinees the audience was almost exclusively goonish, with, perhaps, a sprinkling of jaded women on field trips from suburbia and a few transients up from the bus station.

Of course The Umbrella Lady and The Button Man continued their perfect attendance. Praeger was proud of them. They had, all things considered, adjusted remarkably well—The Umbrella Lady merely surplanted *stupide* with *feelthy* in her critiques, and The Button Man's grin broadened noticeably.

Dewey, the cleaning man, began coming in earlier and earlier each evening until, finally, he was seeing a complete show, properly seated with the audience. Some nights he would leave with the patrons, forgetting to clean up.

Concession business fell off also. Benny Lebowitz grew sullen and cantankerous. Goons had little interest in popcorn or Jujifruits.

Businessmen, conventioneers, salesmen—those familiar with the hard-core versions offered in San Francisco and New York—often complained that all the "goodies" had been cut from the films. They were, indeed, correct. Sometimes only the flagellation and brutality remained. Praeger would have to take them aside and explain the mental workings of The Three Stooges.

Shortly afterward, Gimpelman came up with a new scheme.

He began ordering two prints from the distributors; one going to the censor board for butchering and one to hold back to show intact—bearing the seal assigned the first.

Within a week it was working beyond expectation. The line graph on the bulletin board in Old Man Kane's office spurted upward as business improved; the check machine grew healthy on payday; the tiny red flag denoting the Rococo seemed to glow.

In the evenings at the Rococo, when couples attended, an occasional female would burst into the lobby followed by a perplexed escort. "Well, Christ," he'd be heard mumbling, "I didn't know they were going to show *that*. . . ."

More often than not, though, the couples stayed, coming out flushed and chagrined between shows, some obviously eager to re-enact a few scenes at home.

A film entitled *The Pick Up* was booked. The front office made up schedules and submitted newspaper copy as usual. On the schedules the film was to run seventy minutes. When the print arrived, Waldo Ledbetter discovered it ran ninety minutes. Gimpelman was notified. He sent down simple instructions: cut to conform.

Taking the route of least resistance, and, undoubtedly, realizing his editing would be ineligible for award, Ledbetter lopped off the last reel.

Praeger got on the pay phone in the lobby; the office phone was locked. "You know, Mr. Gimpelman, this thing makes no sense."

"What do you mean makes no sense? Ain't no sex missing is it?"

"How should I know. Nobody's seen the ending."

"Look, them pervs is only interested in sex."

"I've been getting complaints," said Praeger.

"So what's the thing about?"

"Mr. Gimpelman, you're the one who booked it."

"I don't have time to screen everything. What's it about?"

"A porno gangster movie," said Praeger. "These two women steal a suitcase from some Las Vegas money carriers. The carriers go after the women and Las Vegas hoods go after the carriers. . . ."

"And?"

"That's where it ends."

"So what you want me to do, Praeger? Write a new script?"

"Just write a new schedule. I'll have Waldo put the end back on."

"Impossible! Absolutely impossible! Ads are in the paper and everything."

Praeger said nothing for a moment; he merely listened to the erratic breathing coming from Gimpelman's end. "A buck seventy could get the show times changed," he ventured finally, quietly.

"Look, Praeger, you got no business calling me. We got a chain of command around here. You call Winkle next time." He paused an instant, catching breath. "What phone you calling from, anyhow?"

"*Come on*, Mr. Gimpelman, what about it?"

"What about what?"

"The ending."

"Forget it."

"I'll just direct all complaints up to you, all right, Mr. Gimpelman?"

"For Christ's sake! How long you been in this business,

Praeger? Go get a coffee during show breaks. Get a doorman who doesn't speak English. See Lebowitz. He'll show
you how it's done. And while you're at it, get the fuck
off my back!"
The receiver slammed.

After word circulated that unexpurgated sex films were
again being shown at the Rococo, the attorney general
of the state became a steadfast customer. The program
changed every Wednesday, and every Wednesday afternoon he would arrive with a briefcase and a lackey in
tow.
Coming out, walking briskly, he would always have a
comment for the benefit of anyone recognizing him. "We'll
have to see about this one, George," it usually went. "Yes,
we will. Did you get that seal number?"
As if the attorney general had nothing better to do
than check on the Municipal Board of Censors.
He and Praeger soon established a head-nodding ac-
quaintanceship. One morning they ran into each other at
the censor board office; Praeger was there to pick up a
print and the attorney general, obviously, was arriving
for the morning porno screening, briefcase and lackey in
tow.
"Nice weather," he said.

Then there were the ladies of suburbia.
Station wagons full of them, giggling and girdle-bound,
wearing pantsuits from Bloomingdale's and Eau de Paris.
They would enter en masse, troop to the ladies room en
masse, take auditorium seats en masse—none straying
more than two paces from the covey.

Praeger loved them.

When they were in attendance he would take up a post in the lobby at each show break, waiting. As always, out they would file in need of someone to berate, some sounding board for their sweaty-palmed embarrassment, some appeasement for their sweet *coitus interruptus* souls.

Praeger usually made himself available.

Deep in their twittering hearts, he suspected, they wanted to see the most perverse and degenerate of visual happenings, but coming out into stark light with their repressions hanging on them like lanterns, they had to present a façade of indignation.

"Disgusting," they would say, lighting skinny filtered cigarettes. "Such filth shouldn't be shown. *If we'd only known.*"

Early in February someone dropped a dime on the operation (Lebowitz was suspected), and soon afterward the censor board sent an inspector around, court order in hand, authorizing him to confiscate "any and all unlicensed reels of motion picture film."

SUPERDUDE DAY

"Bossman, bossman!" yelled Brother Jason. "They's beat-in' in the side exit on Stricker Street! They's got a crow-bar and hammers and everything. . . ."

Praeger pushed Lebowitz from his path and ran toward the auditorium. He couldn't get through the doorway. The aisles were jammed. He stood to the side and went to his tiptoes. Down front, over rows of heads, he could see two All-Stars standing spread-legged before the gap-ing exit door. They were swinging their billy clubs. He saw them knock a boy to the ground and rip the crowbar from his grip.

After another moment of prodding and jabbing, the guards managed to secure the door. Praeger watched un-til the push bars caught and locked.

"I'd chain 'em shut if it was me," mumbled Lebowitz, elbowing the way to his stand.

Considerately so, he felt, Praeger had initiated a spell of hands-off during Michele's recovery. Despite all her bravado and daring, her chutzpah, her formidable IQ, she was still twenty years old, still but a few seasons out of the nest, and she had been horrendously assaulted. His abstinence soon became a problem. To his mind at least. How might she react when finally his tender cuddlings at night led—and oh how they would—to not-so-tender romps upon the mattress?

She gave no clue.

All of her time was being devoted to her animals. She had quit Kane Theatres. She had dropped out of Godward. She seemed to have small interest in anything beyond the suppering and tendering of her menagerie—which of late included a litter of kittens saved from a drowning sack.

Praeger decided to take a chance. He planned a seduction dinner at home replete with Beaujolais and Bacharach. And, much to his surprise, Michele responded and played her role beautifully through it all—a bit solemn, a bit bruised, a bit martyristic.

After dinner he lowered the music and lit candles in colored-glass urns. Michele wandered around contemplating the collage of movie posters decorating the walls. The male shepherd, Gomer, followed at her feet, a Milk-Bone dog biscuit in his mouth, somewhat cowed by the kittens doing turns over his tail. Ralph, the female sheepdog, could be heard in the kitchen making much racket while stalking a stray cockroach. The sick beagle, as yet unnamed, lay at the foot of the bed watching Fang, an albino parakeet, nose-dive one of the kittens—a retarded thing that was constantly walking into furniture. Michele paused, eyes on Tony Richardson's *Mademoiselle* (Jeanne Moreau kneeling on the ground framed by a man's spread legs). Gomer heeled at her left leg, attentive to a fault.

Praeger moved up behind her and encircled her waist, pressing against her faded denim jeans.

"Dinner was nice," she said.

"Meant it to be." He leaned down, brushed her hair away and kissed the nape of her neck, at the same time slipping his hand under her sweater.

"Cold," she protested, moving away, circling the room. Gomer followed. Then, with a nonchalant toss of her head she settled on the bed and leaned backward, allowing her breasts to press against her sweater, vaguely exposing bumpy nipples.

Praeger flicked off the ceiling light; the room washed pale and eerie—a grainy photograph of dancing candlelight. Steam sputtered from radiator vents, fogging the window. Gently, he lowered himself next to her and kissed her mouth. She parted her lips for him and drew his tongue into play.

"I guess this'll be all right," she said seriously, after a while.

Swapping spearmint saliva with her, he unsnapped her

jeans and began to slide them down. She had to lift her weight from the bed for him to get them below her knees, dropping her shoes in the process. One of them landed on the sick beagle, causing it to grunt and roll over. "Poor baby," said Michele, reaching down to stroke its ears. Gomer, who was famous for his jealousies, came over to the bed to be loved also.

Praeger pulled her sweater over her head, tossing it on the floor. Then he leaned over her and began an easy suckling of her breasts, his right hand caressing her shoulders and nape.

Gomer jumped onto the bed, bringing along his dog biscuit. Several kittens tried to follow but the climb proved too much. Fang, the parakeet, swooped upon a pillow and perched, as if to watch, cocking a nervous head side to side.

Slowly, Praeger moved his mouth over Michele's stomach and thighs, circling, teasing, nibbling—then beneath the elastic band of tricot into copper-tasting folds. She heaved slightly, hands on his shoulders.

Ralph came into the room to see what was going on. She sidled up next to the bed and licked Michele's face. Then she sat down on her haunches and stared, panting audibly, slobbering from the leeward side of her mouth.

"Oh, Ralph," whispered Michele. "You're such a good girl."

Praeger sat up and undressed, all the while caressing Michele with one hand and intermittently petting Gomer with the other.

Michele slipped out of her panties and dropped them on the carpet. They were immediately pounced upon by the kittens, tugging and tossing, backing then, attacking, clawing, and ripping.

"Do it nice," she said, looking up at him.

"Yes, yes, yes . . ." He moved over her and entered gently, his hands cupping the flesh of her buttocks, lifting her up to meet him.

Ralph continued snuggling her face. "Poor Baldy," she whimpered. "Too bad he can't be here."

Slowly at first, savoring her, adjusting to her particular sway and cant—as all women are different if one took the time to discover it and never would he believe otherwise —Praeger began a concerted movement of pelvis and hip, which soon wavered into vacillation, and then abandonment. . . .

"Hold me, hold me tight," said Michele.

Fang hopped from the pillow and landed on Praeger's posterior, pecking at dog biscuit crumbs sticking to his skin. He was in no position to swat him away. It would break the mood for Michele. So he let him peck.

Gomer climbed down long enough to shit on the rug.

The sick beagle opened her eyes and wagged her tail. Ralph curled up amid a pile of Praeger's discarded clothing. Kittens scampered about the room, tumbling and leaping, dancing over the floor on soft, silent pads.

"Oh, nice," Michele mumbled. "Oh, so nice . . ."

Gomer, atop the bed once more, began jumping about, barking, nuzzling Praeger and Michele, thinking some grand game had been devised for his playtime.

SUPERDUDE DAY

Praeger paid a visit to Superdude.

The claque of nurses had him cornered behind Teddy Winkle's desk. Their faces were flushed. Two of them had removed most of their clothing. White slips and girdles and brassieres were draped about as if a bargain basement sale was in progress. Teddy Winkle's papers were strewn about the floor. Chairs were upturned. Superdude, batting them away, wore a frightful expression. "M'man, m'man," he pleaded, "get me out of here."

"Time to pay dues, Superdude."

"Like, *huh?*"

"Step aside, ladies," said Praeger, exposing the monstrous revolver.

The nurses began screeching. "He got a gun, he got a gun!" They grabbed their clothing and pocketbooks and stampeded the door. One of them clutched his arm. "Don't shoot us, mister."

Trailing his cape, Superdude ducked low and spurted behind them. He paused long enough to survey the murderous commotion below, then turned and made for the balcony. A few youngsters recognized him and tried to stop him, but he pushed past, through the hallway and arch, finally inside.

118

Then, all at once, he paused in midstride. "Oh, my Lawd!" he gasped.

On screen, Vita Vibes was making slurping sounds with her mouth wrapped around a huge purple penis.

Praeger followed.

The air inside the balcony was oppressive. Cigarette smoke mixed with a civetlike stench, the fetor of the ghetto, clouded under the ceiling. Moving in and out of aisles, Praeger began coughing, heaving for breath. Then, looking up, rows above him, in the flickering cascade of light coming from the projection booth, he picked out the black cape of Superdude flowing across the top most landing of the balcony.

Two women blocked Praeger's way. He mumbled an apology and nudged them aside. A hand grabbed his arm. Curses followed. He exposed the revolver and cocked it. The hand released him.

Thanks to Vita Vibes, Superdude had gotten through the audience without being recognized.

Praeger skipped steps two at a stride until he reached the spot where he had seen him. He then stood panting, eyes darting at the slightest movement. The cape was gone from sight. He searched every seat and face. Nothing.

Over his shoulder a wash of light caught his attention. The back hallways!

He wheeled and ran toward them. Through a kicked-open door he could see dozens of people wandering up and down the halls. Offices had been pried open also. Men were sitting about in clusters drinking gin and wine from paper sacks.

Teen-age boys went room to room rifling file cabinets;

others slouched about thumbing through press books and promo material, gawking at releases from X-rated films.

"The Man's here!" cried the lookout. "The Man's here!"

"Fuck the Man."

Praeger paused, surveying the hallway. His eyes locked on a torpedo trash can. It seemed to be covered with hair. Then he realized it was covered with Superdude's cape. And behind Superdude's cape, no doubt thinking he was hidden, crouched Superdude.

Cringing, two maroon eyes peeped around the side of the can.

Seeing the drawn handgun, Superdude jumped up and backed off. Praeger raised the weapon and aimed it. Superdude spun on the balls of his feet and dashed away. He jumped a barricade of discarded furniture and scurried on hands and knees up a stairway, leaving a trail of fur.

Praeger went after him.

At the top, Superdude stumbled into another hallway —this one deserted and filth-strewn, lit only by a cracked skylight. A cul-de-sac. He backed against a boarded door. A frantic plea distended his features. Praeger walked toward him, revolver cocked, pointed at the famous and soon-to-be immortal face of Lorenzo Jones.

A.k.a. Superdude.

"Wait, m'man, wait!" he began babbling. "I'll go on! I'll go on! Anything you say, m'man. You're my main man."

Gimpelman tried another experiment which lasted three days and ended for all time sexploitation at the Rococo.

A 16 mm projector was set up in the balcony and Teddy Winkle was given a crash course in its operation. Then, Teddy Winkle's paperwork and desk lamp were moved to the loge, where Gimpelman stationed him all day showing reels of blue movies, plus doing his own work.

Teddy Winkle loved it. Especially viewing the Danish imports where the starring creature was, more often than not, a natural blonde.

As a precaution, a buzzer system was wired between the box office and the projection booth. If Ida—who knew everyone—saw anything unkosher on the street, she would signal the booth and Ledbetter would go on screen with the regular 35 mm feature—and, of course, Teddy Winkle would cut the 16 mm.

On a rainy, chilling-to-the-bone Wednesday, the system debuted. Ida saw two hard-noses from the vice squad slipping in to get warm.

She dutifully buzzed Ledbetter.

Ledbetter struck his carbons and went on with the second reel of the censored feature—a relatively mild sequence of a nymphet playing suggestively with a candle-stick.

Unfortunately, Teddy Winkle was not in the balcony; the 16 mm projector was running unattended. Watching the films had made him so horny he had gone to his office to call one of his blonde girl friends for a date—a pug-nosed, simple-minded giglet, but a sure lay when primed with dinner and three screwdrivers. By the time Ledbetter stumbled down to shut the machine off it was too late. Superimposed in grainy black and white over the candlestick scene was a buxom lovely being fucked by a donkey.

The vice squad officers called for a wagon.

Sitting in the audience at the time of the raid was the attorney general and his lackey. Filing out past the police line, he explained to the ranking officer—blossoming with embarrassment—that he was conducting his own investigation and that his office was prepared to cooperate with the city police to the utmost.

Teddy Winkle, Ledbetter, and Hawkes, who was managing at the time, spent the night in Central's lockup. Tongue-in-cheek, the local papers gave the incident front page billing; the story also went out over the AP wire. Teddy Winkle's picture appeared coast to coast. It showed him grinning and waving his hand from behind bars, stripped down to a Mickey Mouse T-shirt.

Pickets from the Action Committee for Decency showed up in front of the Rococo the next day with placards. The distributor of the film supposedly being shown called Gimpelman from New York—they were suing. The state's attorney's office prepared an indictment upon urgings from one of the Rococo's former foremost customers, Attorney General Louis Tassone. The projectionists' local staged a wildcat strike.

Gimpelman went into seclusion.

30

Praeger could put it off no longer.

The cleaning man—molelike Dewey—had come to see him about it in person, in stark daylight. Ledbetter mentioned it again. He had even begun seeing them himself: shadows aft of the screen.

Someone *was* backstage.

His imagination began conjuring up visions, phantasmagoric images—and time and again the mental picture he formed was that of Michele's pelted rapist, a black apparition lurking in the folds of dusty curtains.

Then, to make the challenge even more spectral, the atmosphere diabolical, Gimpelman began booking foreign films. Bergmans and Godards. Spidery, black-cloaked figures of Death stalking cliffsides. Endless pan shots and surreal monologues. Mordant humor, good struggling evil, curses galore weighed under the efficacy of godly miracles.

Suddenly, the Rococo was an art house.

Everyone thought Gimpelman had suffered the mental breakdown often predicted for him. Then they realized it was a ploy for the court.

The obscenity case was going to be heard before the

bench of the Honorable S. Rodrick Pearce, a known film buff who wrote extensively on the subject for small journals and all but lived in the art houses up in Guinness Village.

Unfortunately for Gimpelman and the crisis at hand, the art houses in Guinness Village were run by a small reputable chain and had nothing to do with Kane Theatres.

Gimpelman was desperate. It was his second offense within weeks.

He tried hanging an exhibit of oil paintings in the lobby like the Guinness Village theatres did—but half were stolen within two days. He proposed serving free coffee like the Guinness Village theatres did—but Benny Lebowitz went berserk, ranting and screaming: "Free?! Free?! What are you, a fucking communist? Nothing's *ever* free at my stands!" He talked about having comfortable swayback seats like the Guinness Village theatres did, but the expense, of course, was prohibitive; then Praeger pointed out that half the seats in the Rococo were already swayback—they were broken.

Again, business dropped to the ludicrous.

The whole episode was summed up perfectly by two black boys coming out five minutes after all the hassle of sneaking in the back: "What kind of jive shit is this? Those motherfuckers can't speak no English!"

Tuesday night, with Bertolucci's *The Spider's Stratagem* playing, with eight people in the audience, Praeger decided it was time he investigated backstage. He took a crowbar from the janitor's supply room and a flashlight from his office. His plan was simple. Use one of his secret passageways. Approach backstage from the balcony where he wouldn't be seen, where no one could lay a trap for him. Then, quietly, hide in the darkness and wait.

Wait for the shadows.

Going through the lobby with his paraphernalia he was stopped by Brother Jason, eyeing the crowbar. "You gonna have a chat with that Mr. Lebowitz?" he asked. He was grinning wart to wart.

"I'm going to have a chat with somebody," said Praeger, plodding up the Grand Staircase.

Entering the balcony he chose a locked door along the west wall, secluded behind a bank of frayed curtains. It was painted black. It looked as if no one had touched it in the months since he'd used it last.

He turned the cylinder lock and pushed. It swung open to expose a passage, a landing, and then a descent. Air gushed up to meet him. Musty-smelling. Chilling. He had activated a vacuum—some forbidden leecock in the balance of drafts and currents—and once through the passageway it took all his might to pull the door shut.

Shivering, he steadied himself on the landing for a moment. Then he flicked on the flashlight, illuminating his path along a narrow stairway, unusually long, steps constructed but inches apart, dropping in a horizontal flow toward backstage.

He tightened his grip on the crowbar and started down. If he remembered correctly he would come out just to the rear of the screen.

At the bottom, he cracked the door and waited for a dark scene from Bertolucci. Then he entered as quietly as possible, edging along a corridor formed between the screen and mountains of refuse. He felt the way with his fingers. Midway behind the screen he found a spot among wooden crates. It faced the dressing rooms.

Suddenly, an eerie musical score erupted from wall speakers. The scene on the screen brightened. Spears of green foliage rippled across his skin and clothing. He looked up. He could see scaffolding reaching to the ceiling among draping ropes and ominous-looking bags of sand hanging as counterweights. He could see the faint light of the street seeping through cracks in boarded windows.

He sank into his enclave. The floor was icy. Chills leapt through him. He felt all at once vulnerable and fervidly impatient.

On screen, inverted to Praeger, as if he had seeped from the scenario, the film's antifascist hero was strutting about in bush jacket and slicked hair. . . .

He snapped into a wide-eyed stare.

A sound reached him. From one of the dressing rooms. A light had switched on. Third room from the west wall. He could see the yellowish stream beneath the door, shimmering the stage floor toward him.

He forced himself to sit still. His heart pounded inside his jacket. A rancid taste covered his tongue. Finally, he tried to stand. His legs wouldn't move. They felt weighed with ballast.

Oh, Jesus Christ! He rubbed them. He pounded them. He could feel a cramp taking hold, twisting sinew and muscle. He bit down on his lip. Drawing blood. Then, mercifully, the pain began to recede.

He hooked the crowbar over one of the crates and pulled himself up. He massaged his legs, shaking one

foot at a time, moving out a step or two. Fingering his
keys, he limped across the stage to the door. Its surface
was scarred and smudged where decades of hand prints
had deposited indelible layers of grime. He put an ear
against it and listened. Nothing. Not a sound. He slipped
the master key into the lock and turned.

Then he pushed.

The door held firm. He turned the key again. Then
again. All the while pushing. Still it refused to budge.
Quickly, he checked for other locks, for latches, for
nailed boards, for anything that could be securing it.

Nothing.

Then, sticking the flashlight and crowbar under his
belt, he raised his foot and kicked. The door rocked in
its frame but held. He whispered curses to himself, bat-
tering it again. Finally, gasping for breath, sweating, he
slumped back against the crates.

The light from beneath the door washed across his
shoes. He tried again, this time turning the knob with
his left hand and heaving with his body weight.

It groaned and screeched and gave an inch.

Another push and it popped open. Swinging wide.
Banging the wall. He lifted his crowbar and stood within
the doorframe. His heart bobbed into his throat like a
cork in water.

Under stark light, at a desk covered with old press
books and faded news clippings, sat an impeccably
dressed man, looking directly at him.

"Hello, lad, I'm Mr. Max."

IV

MISTER MAX

31

"Lad, don't just stand there," said the man at the desk. "Come in." He was small and wiry, silver-haired, fine featured, dapper in dress—much unlike what Praeger expected from a figure stepped from legend.

Praeger stared at him like a dunderhead. "What are you doing here?" He could feel a slack-jawed, incredulous look seeping through his own face.

"You've heard my name before, I imagine?"

"Yes, of course I've heard it."

The little man's eyes twinkled. "Then who better should be here? Who with more right to be in the Rococo Theatre?"

Praeger had no answer. "I'm the manager," he said feebly, an afterthought.

"I know who you are. Clinton Praeger, isn't it?"

"Clifton," said Praeger.

"Clinton Clifton?"

"No, Praeger."

"Clinton Clifton Praeger?"

Praeger shrugged. "That's close enough," he said. His voice was strangely husky. Foreign and far-sounding to his own ear. He cleared his throat and forced himself to speak. "You still haven't told me why you're back here. What's going on."

The man sat absolutely still; he seemed to be barely drawing a breath. "I come every day."

"For God's sake, what for?"

"It's my theatre, Clinton."

"It's a Kane Theatre."

"RKO, Silberman, Kane—what's it matter who's holding the lease. They come, they go. It's still my theatre. My building—"

"I thought it was sold."

"—if not in deed, in spirit."

Jesus, Praeger thought at that instant, *I'm not going to believe any of this in the morning.*

"Come here, come here, lad. I'll show you history books like you've never imagined. All about my theatre. She's like a ship, you know. A beautiful, sleek ship fallen upon stormy days. But I'm her master. I love her. And I won't desert her now."

Praeger looked at him and grimaced. *The old guy's crackers.*

John Maximillian wasn't always crazy.

He had been born (mental facilities intact) on the morning of ground breaking for the Rococo Theatre. Both events were given due notice in the evening paper of that day. And both were largely ignored by the public—a public with no hint of a certain astrological kinship, far beyond coincidence, linking the respective births.

Two years earlier the Maximillians had toured Europe with three of their five children, a secretary, a nanny, and an entourage of advisers and hangers-on. In London, the elder Mr. Max, known to all as Million Max, was so taken with a particularly good season of English theatre that he vowed on the spot—which happened to be a pub off the Strand—to provide his own stateside metropolis with its equal.

He engaged an architect, a Londoner who had made a name designing West End theatres, and had the man dispatched to the States to inspect sites and begin drawings. A full city block was finally chosen. The standing buildings, which included the municipal car barn and stables, were purchased and razed.

Certain antagonists spread rumors that Million Max's motives were neither aesthetic nor civic. He had, they maintained, conceived his mammoth theatre in order to

133

lure to the United States a certain acting troupe that included a young raven-haired girl of extraordinary beauty by the name of Karen Read.

If the rumors had truth, Million Max accomplished his mission. The theatre was built. The troupe came. His wife, a frail and retiring matron who never completely recovered from the state of childbearing so late in life, died soon afterward on a rainy August night.

It was as if the hand of destiny had taken Million Max upon its palm.

John Maximillian was fifteen months old at the time of his mother's death; shortly afterward he had a raven-haired stepmother.

Karen Read Maximillian was poor replacement for a matriarch. But John seemed not to notice or care. Unlike his siblings, he remembered no other mother—in fact, *wished* to remember no other mother.

The English beauty had an insatiable love for all humanity, all creatures great and small. She abhorred cruelty and, being too sensitive for her own well-being, was known to bang her fist into walls, known to shatter china, and known to shed a tear.

She managed passably in running the household, but in no way was she about to become a quiet obedient wife. Million Max realized her spirit and gave her rein aplenty. About town she became a bold defender of lost causes, she smoked cigarettes, she dressed and wore her hair differently from other women, she was often argumentative with men, but mostly her energies were spent maintaining a not-so-secret passion for the theatre.

And John, without benefit of genetics, inherited it.

SUPERDUDE DAY

Praeger locked himself in Teddy Winkle's office with Superdude.

"Sit down over there and rehearse," he ordered, motioning the black man toward Lebowitz's cubbyhole. "And rehearse good—because, my friend, when you get on stage you better dazzle them."

Superdude appeared ill. He looked up at Praeger, who was even taller than himself, although not as hefty, and certainly not the together dude he was. He thought for a moment of making a move for him, giving him a karate chop, Kung Fu-ing the gun away. Then he realized the one small fact preventing him: *This was no fucking movie.*

He went to the corner and sat down.

Praeger scanned the room. The three buttons on Teddy Winkle's desk phone were lit and blinking; the local buzzer was sounding an extended lament. It was, he figured, as good a place as any to keep Superdude secured until showtime.

"Yeah!" he said, snatching up the receiver.

"What'll I do? What'll I do? I'm on the last reel of *Sucko.*" It was Ledbetter. Machines could be heard running in the background. Obviously, it had dawned

135

on Ledbetter just what was going on. And he was in a panic. "Only thirteen minutes left. What'll I do when it ends? I ain't got nothing more here but a *Willy Wonka* trailer and a Marine Corps training short. What'll I do?"

"Turn on the house lights, put a spot center stage, and say your rosary."

34

It was a grand piece of work upon being put up, this Rococo Theatre. It had 2,000,000 bricks, 800 tons of art plaster and lime, 180 tons of steel, 500,000 feet of channel iron, 20,000 yards of metal lath, 50 tons of modeling clay, 300,000 feet of galvanized tie wire. . . .

Grand and awesome.

Audiences were at once struck with a maze of Rose du Barri draperies, gilt candelabras, handrails and plinth in antique, balustrades of alabaster, steps of veined marble. Stepping into the auditorium was a breath-rendering experience. Its size was staggering. Attending a performance was akin to watching Meissen-like figurines promenading about a puppet-show setting.

Four tiers faced the stage—stalls, dress circle, grand tier, and gallery. Six private boxes were located on either side of the proscenium and the proscenium arch was covered with elaborate bas-relief groupings.

The saucer-domed ceiling, an exact duplication of one so admired in London by Million Max, was ornamented with symbolic carvings depicting "Endeavor," "The Light of the World," "Love," "The Crowning Success," and "The Torch of Destiny."

An opening night critic was moved to comment in summation: "Do attend, and do bring binoculars."

Yet, despite superb productions imported by Million Max, the theatre was never a success under his hand. Its very enormousness, its relatively small stage, and its admittedly poor acoustics—not to mention absolute deaf spots—were blamed.

Million Max died in 1906. His young wife inherited a large family, blocks of real estate, bonds and stocks, and several hundred thousand dollars in cash. Wanting the Rococo to remain in her control, she leased it to theatrical acquaintances over her attorney's suggestion that she sell it.

In March, 1907, a new regime began at the Rococo under Scott and Sloane Associates, presenting "good drama at fair prices." The innards of the theatre were entirely rebuilt. The boxes were removed. The stage was widened by ten feet. A more spacious entrance foyer was created. Ornamental carvings and a number of statues were introduced into the decor, which by now defied all definition. A low-relief bust of Shakespeare, snuggled between Comedy and Tragedy, was mounted over the principal entrance.

Scott and Sloane managed to pay the rent month to month—but nothing else.

In 1916 the lease passed to Adelbaum Attractions, who presented, among other disasters, a revue called *Beer For My Dear*, followed by *Spinning Carousels*. Unfortunately, these efforts also failed at the box office.

No durable reputation had yet been established for the Rococo. Audiences were never quite sure what they would see. It was often embarrassing to performers and management alike when the most serious productions were attended by giggling foursomes thinking they were to see variety skits, or worse, when society matrons were faced with burlesque.

A strange mixture of plays, revues, musicals, and vaudeville occupied the stage until the summer of 1922 when Karen Read Maximillian reassumed the lease for her youngest stepson. Two weeks after graduation from Cooper Union and twenty-one years of age, John Maximillian took over the Rococo.

From that day he was known as Mr. Max.

From Boston to San Francisco, movie "cathedrals" were opening as fast as they could be financed and built. The country was aswarm with Bijoux and Cameos, Rivolis and Gems. Vaudeville was waning. The nickelodeon days of converted stores and traveling tent shows were gone; New York alone had a thousand movie houses.

Mr. Max sensed what was coming. And he meant for the Rococo to be part of it.

He installed a projection booth and motion picture screen. He entered into a contractual agreement with William Matlock Associates, the respected talent agency in New York. His idea was simple: match topnotch vaudeville with a studio feature at a popular price.

Very soon, without even inquiring about the stage bill or picture, patrons became confident that every show change at the Rococo would be worth the trek downtown.

It took Mr. Max but two months to accomplish what had been attempted for a quarter of a century: the books showed black.

By late 1927 the talkie boom had swept the larger cities, and it was announced by Mr. Max that the Rococo was to be wired for sound.

Instead of opening with *The Jazz Singer,* which was, in his words, "a squawking schmaltz of a film," Mr. Max waited for something with sound and *substance.*

None came.

Mr. Max premièred his new Vitaphone equipment by refusing to use it. The statement he made at the time was widely reprinted:

"Motion pictures have developed a rare and subtle beauty of late—by their very silence. They've become so fluid and magically adept at telling their stories by visual means that the Rococo will continue to show silent films. Our aim is to provide the finest entertainment available. When the Vitaphone process provides something more than tacked-on gibberish—all for the sake of commercialism—we will add them to our bookings."

Coupled with Janet Gaynor in *Seventh Heaven* on a mute screen, George Jessel played a record ten weeks as master of ceremonies to the finest array of skit artists, stand-up comedians, and song and dance teams assembled in the city before or since, all for twenty-five cents before six, forty cents after.

And so began the golden days at the Rococo.

Mr. Max saw to it that an afternoon in his theatre was the best-spent two bits on the East Coast. In fact, Mr. Max saw to everything. Operating from his office atop the Grand Staircase, he left nothing to chance. His staff was well-paid. Bonuses were frequent—even during the bleakest Depression years. He was a good boss. As good,

said those in the business, as "Roxy" Rothafel himself,
the great theatre entrepreneur in New York.

A popular man in local social enclaves, Mr. Max had
many friends and many connections. He sat on several
prestigious boards. He escorted beautiful women to
sporting events and he dined at the homes of important
politicians and business leaders.

Until he went "crazy."

On July 2, 1938, he announced that henceforth persons
of color were welcome at the Rococo Theatre. The day
proved both prideful and heart-sating for Karen Read
Maximillian, who lay at the time on her deathbed.

SUPERDUDE DAY

Herman Kane received the call from Union General Hospital. His general manager, Sidney Gimpelman, had been admitted with multiple, although unspecified, fractures. He had also lost much blood. And a couple of teeth.

But he would live.

Herman Kane slammed the phone down and began yelling for his secretary. He wanted to be lifted from his swivel chair. He wanted his overcoat fetched. And he wanted his walking stick.

He was going over to the Rococo. He was going to take personal charge of Superdude Day.

Praeger and Michele lay together in bed. It was three o'clock in the morning. Praeger couldn't sleep.

"Strangest damn feeling . . . watching him just sit and talk like his being there was the most natural thing in the world."

Michele yawned. "Maybe it is."

"He's got no business inside. The Maximillians lost everything in the Depression. Too generous, it seems. The new owners threw him out on his ass soon afterward. And they'd have hallooed him out of town if they'd been smart."

Gutsy old bastard, Praeger mumbled to himself, his mind flip-flopping, enthralled with the story he'd become privy to earlier. The recent comings and goings, he had learned, were by a secret back exit, a passageway designed personally by Million Max for name performers to flee unmolested—or for discreet visits to the dressing room area by a certain gentleman.

After losing his position, finding himself persona non grata at the front door, Mr. Max took up using the clandestine entrance. He couldn't stay away. Within hours on the day of his first visit, after moping about backstage amid echoes of a shoot-em-up Western, he realized,

143

very simply, that he had no intention of giving up his theatre.

Someone, he had told himself, would be needed to continue the press books, to record and preserve the new era, be it grand or shysterly. And he decided he was that someone.

So, clipping by clipping, day by day, every word of print about the Rococo—every ad, every calendar listing, every handout, every review of every film that played —fell under his paste brush.

"Are you sleeping?" asked Michele.

"No."

"I am."

He must have sat at that desk, Praeger thought, all of those years, snipping and pasting, unbeknown to anyone, until this very night.

It was unearthly, indeed.

Yet, to Praeger's mind, many things began to make sense. For every file cabinet dumped backstage by Lebowitz or Gimpelman, Mr. Max had come out ferretlike to gather the remains, retreating to dress wounds, to reconstruct the material in chronological volumes. *God, the man's pertinacity!* The dated and bound scrapbooks —each half a foot thick—were stacked by the dozens in his shadowy room, with the current one lying open on his desk.

"I can't get over it," said Praeger. "It was like some telepathy was going on between us . . . like he was this *force*, you see . . . giving off vibrations."

"Vibrations?" said Michele, stirring. "What do you mean?"

"I don't know. I think maybe . . . I guess he's the old. And I'm the new. And I'm really fucking up—"

"As usual."

"I'm serious. Can't you see that?"

Gomer, the shepherd, climbed up between them.

"Do you know what he said was coming?" Praeger added. After waiting for a response but getting nothing other than the sound of her breathing, he continued, if only to hear himself say it. "Blaxploitation."

"*Huh?*"

"Black Gary Coopers and white Stepin Fetchits."

Michele yawned and rolled sideward, her arm draping the dog. "I think you've both seen too many movies."

SUPERDUDE DAY

Lebowitz brought in two extra hot dog rotisseries and a large electrically operated tub from the Eagle. The tub, when filled with water, was plugged into one of the extension cords hanging like jungle vines over the stand. Lights dimmed in the lobby. Sparks sputtered from a wall receptacle. Lebowitz gave the tub a hefty kick, then began dumping boxes of frozen hot dogs into the water.

Concession business had been phenomenal all morning. Benny Lebowitz's skin shone under an ecstatic sweat. He had never seen anything like it. *A bloody dream!* The people were captive. The people were famished. The people had money.

They crowded ten abreast, like squealing piglets, thrusting sawbucks across the glass. Benny Lebowitz had called in every available girl—and they in turn stood three abreast taking orders, fixing orders, thrusting back folding cardboard trays full of goodies.

The fat man hovered behind, rubbing his body against the girls' asses, stuffing paper money into a Super Saver shopping bag, tossing change into a scrub bucket.

His only problem seemed to be Praeger. Praeger paid no attention to anything he said.

He was losing a fortune. Street urchins were sneaking

146

in the exits, filtering up to his stand, pushing aside paying customers, seeing what they could pilfer in the confusion. The exits had to be chained. Yet he knew it would
mean a confrontation with Praeger. And Praeger was
toting a gun.

Gun or not, the man was incompetent. Lebowitz real-
ized it was up to him to take charge. Someone had to.
He left his money long enough to order a dullard of an
All-Star to chain every exit. Then, he let himself into
Praeger's office and pocketed the ring of exit keys.

The overgrown simpleton's not going to unchain them
this time, he thought, bullying back to the stand.

The Button Man never spoke. He communicated by pointing to various tin messages covering his clothing. His vocabulary was, if nothing else, bizarre.

I Made Vita Vibes Gag.

Praeger cornered him next morning on the frozen sidewalk outside the theatre. He brought up the subject of Mr. Max, asking if he'd ever noticed him around the theatre. The Button Man gave a pained stare, hesitated, then walked away, trailing a stream of icy breath.

Obviously, there was no button for the occasion.

Half an hour later The Umbrella Lady informed Praeger that Mr. Max had died in a hotel fire in 1947. She even named the cemetery where his remains lay.

Praeger sat in his office the rest of the morning bending paper clips.

"Fuckass grave should be right here. Right here. What propafuckinganda is this? Chart says right here. Look for yourself."

Praeger grimaced. He and the gnomish caretaker were standing in the median strip of a two-lane highway which intersected St. John's Cemetery.

"I know the problem. I know." He tapped Praeger's arm and motioned for him to follow. They retraced their path across the highway's southbound lane. Angry car horns sounded, swishing past in prolonged drones. "Fuck you, you creeps!" screamed the gnome. "Ain't you got no respect for the dead!" Up a weed-covered slope they crawled, among broken glass and discarded tires, then through a hole in a barbed-wire fence. "Sure you ain't come about the gravedigger job I got in the newspaper?"

"Afraid not," said Praeger, wishing he'd worn a suit instead of a turtleneck and old corduroy pants—anything to convince the man he wasn't for hire as a laborer. "Just like to look at this Maximillian marker, that's all."

"Gonna be all autofuckinmated now."

"What?"

"Gonna do our digging by machine—except we still need a few men for touchup, you know. Gonna be easier than digging in horseshit now. Don't have to be too particular anyhow. Ain't nothin but niggers and winos gets buried down here anymore. City pays for them. Used to be a fair place till these punk kids started using it for boozin' and screwin'. Be truthful with you, it ain't worth a healthy do-do. Imfuckinpossible even to find a plot. What markers the punks ain't kicked over, the city's done run a road through. Expressway coming next year, right through here."

Praeger said nothing as they tread through the acidic urban atmosphere. Soot sheeted the earth like a fine gray snow. Across rows of askew markers he could see—between factory smoke towers—patches of scum-coated harbor and rusted hulls of scraped ships.

"You're big and strong enough," the gnome said.

"Pardon?"

"For grave diggin'."

"Look, I'm not interested. Really."

"Better off I guess. Fancy fuckinass funeral directors and them hired stooge drivers make all the fuckin' money anyhow."

They reached the office again: a small stuccoed building with cinder-block windows ornamented by narrow gun slits. The man opened the series of locks and double doors he had secured just minutes earlier. Inside, furnishings consisted of a desk, file cabinet, chair, and wall phone; in the rear, through an open door, Praeger could see a toilet closet, its walls papered with split-beavers cut from Danish magazines.

"So where's Maximillian buried?"

"Well," the gnome lisped, throwing open a frayed

ledger. "Two things coulda happened, my friend. De-scendants coulda claimed him or the city coulda exhumed and reinterred his ass somewheres else around here."

"What about your chart?"

The man shot him an annoyed look. He reminded Praeger of those anonymous, quietly deranged figures one always ran across in all-night eateries.

"Well?"

"Give me a chance to look, will you." The man bent over the ledger, squinting. "Let's see . . . Maximillian . . . Maximillian . . . looks like we ain't got no listing of no Maximillian being reinterred. You sure he's suppose to be here?"

"*For Christ's sake!* You told me on the phone he was here. You've got a record of him on your chart."

"That old thing ain't much accurate."

"Well, *somebody* should have a record of him!"

"All right. All right. I only fuckin' work here. I don't own the place, you know. My name ain't St. John, you know. You come around here looking for some stiff been dead God knows how long? Not only that, but his ass happens to be planted right in the wrong place. Right where the highway went through the old section. Them clowns down there been stonefuckindead for years. When'd he die anyhow?"

"Your ledger should have told us that," he said.

"Well, it dint," said the gnome.

Praeger hesitated, then said, "Sometime back in the forties."

"You sure seem anxious. You a relative?"

"No."

The gnome looked at him suspiciously. "Well, what's your game? What's hot shit about this Maximillian guy anyhow?"

"He's just a man I'm researching."

"*Researching?*"

"That's right. Anything wrong with that? I want to see the grave. I want to touch the stone. I want to read the inscription. I want to kick the mound of earth. I want to know if there really is a grave. *I've got to know if he's there.*"

The man stood dumbfounded. "Where else would he be?"

"You tell me."

"Look, mister, I'll be honest. I'll tell you what I think happened. If'n the marker was knocked down or gone, and if'n weeds were grown around, them city people probably built their highway right over him. Been known to happen, you know."

"Are you serious?"

"Dead serious." Sheepishly, the man lifted his round, froglike eyes. He seemed vaguely aware of being caught with a pun on his tongue.

Praeger began mumbling to himself.

"That's why I'm gonna have my ass cremated. Yes sir, ain't gonna be shuffled around for no Godfuckindamn expressways, that's for sure. Not me. They got this new thing now. Up in New York. Economy Cremations. Do the whole bit for two hundred and sixty-five dollars. Keep you in a can or scatter your ashes. Don't matter. Same price."

"*JesusfuckinChrist!*" Praeger heard himself say, before turning to flee, ducking his head under the doorframe, stepping among toppled markers and jungles of winter-brown weed.

The gnome called after him, jumping up and down. "Where you going? You hear me. Where you going? I want to talk to you about that diggin job. . . ."

During the next week, Praeger went backstage almost every night hoping to see Mr. Max again—or at least the person claiming to be Mr. Max—but each visit found the room padlocked and dark.

No one but Michele knew about his discovery.

He dared not mention it to anyone at the Rococo; they all thought he was loony enough already.

"You're supposed to be dead, Mr. Max," he shouted into the silent auditorium one night after closing. "Do you hear me? Everyone thinks you're dead."

Mice scurried among the aisles, a dog in the back alley began barking, but no human sound came back, other than a mocking echo.

BLACK ACTION

Business was worse than ever.

Kane Theatres laid off all nonessential employees. Ushers. Maintenance men. Payroll clerks. Secretaries. Cashiers. Relief managers. Candy girls. Janitors.

Heat was ordered cut back in all houses. So severe was the chill inside that doormen took up wearing mackinaws. Then, shortly afterward, a directive came down from the front office instructing everyone that wearing heavy coats, blowing on hands, stamping feet, or drinking coffee would not be tolerated. To the best of their ability, they were to make the theatres appear warm inside.

157

Gimpelman was all at once a law-abiding fanatic. He wasn't having the WALK—DON'T RUN TO YOUR NEAREST EXIT snippet run without a censor's seal.

Also, with *The Spider's Stratagem* leaving, so too went his art house pretensions. They had done little good. The obscenity case had come and gone, leaving Kane Theatres with a fine for three thousand dollars plus legal expenses—and leaving Gimpelman in a blue funk. He wanted to hear no mention of the Rococo. He hated the very sound of the word. Especially the perverse way it seemed to dribble from one's tongue.

He took a week off, flying unexpectedly to Miami with a woman other than his wife, leaving Teddy Winkle stuck with bookings.

Inspired with his new authority, Teddy Winkle went on a mental booking binge. He thought he would have an Our Gang comedy film festival (they were his favorites), but a local TV station had beat him to it a week earlier. Then he thought of a Charlie Chan festival. Or a Randolph Scott festival. Or a Fatty Arbuckle festival. Anything he could pick up cheap.

Gimpelman had left no money in the booking account.

Casablanca doubled with *The Maltese Falcon* perhaps. *Golddiggers of 1933* and *Footlight Parade*.

As luck would have it, though, he found something better, something cheaper, something from a small distributor in New York who had no idea they weren't about to receive payment. He booked an old horror combo: the original 1931 version of Tod Browning's *Freaks* (emasculation scene intact) and *The White Zombie* with Bela Lugosi.

Something strange happened at the Rococo that week.

Blacks began to purchase tickets. Ghetto blacks. Drifting out from the barbed-wire-encircled projects and doorless row houses with the smog-grey stoops.

Word-of-mouth was bringing them. Out of the shantytown barrooms and the cement basketball courts they came, in tenners and headrags, in platforms and berets —a phalanx of blackamoors. It was great fun for them, it seemed, watching all the deformed, gargoylish creatures in *Freaks*. Great fun because all the deformed, gargoylish creatures in *Freaks* were honkies.

The White Zombie was explanatory enough by title.

Teddy Winkle, all the while, hadn't the vaguest notion as to what was going on; he was flabbergasted when black faces began to show at Ida's box office. The floppy Three Musketeer hats and Afro hair styles and dashikis puzzled him no end. All he had done was book the cheapest hunk of shit he could find.

The new patrons were nervous, apprehensive. Upon entering, quiet and clannish, most trudged immediately to the back-of-the-bus of theatredom: the balcony. Finding it barred and disused, they then wandered back down the Grand Staircase to the auditorium, taking poor seats in side rows. Crossing the lobby en route, their faces held wary looks—half defiant, half cringing—as if they expected loud-speakers to suddenly peal out, ordering them elsewhere.

But they were wrong.

Other than a lanky manager and a few urban crazies, whitey wasn't about. The place, this long-forbidden downtown palace, had fallen to them like some abandoned fortress, and it was taking them no time to claim the spoils. Soon they were roaming about the building like drunken sailors, free to reconnoiter, to visit its rest rooms, flush its toilets, primp before its mirrors, meander its concourses, its lobbies, its stairways and rotundas.

All at once they were moving to choice center seats in the orchestra. Lighting up cigarettes. Cheering and stomping. Pursuing conversations between rows as if partying in someone's living room, drink in hand.

Then they discovered the concession stand.

Benny Lebowitz couldn't believe how they feasted. He immediately jacked up prices. They didn't care. They wanted more. He added fried chicken and barbecued ribs. French fries and ice cream. Potato chips and Super-Cola. They bought it by the armloads. They gobbled it up. The taboo atmosphere, the ornate surroundings urged them to splurge, to spend their welfare dollars in high style at this obviously class joint where food stamps meant naught.

Oh, you sweet people, where have you been! Lebowitz breathed to himself, jabbing frankfurters on rotisserie hooks.

Rested and suntanned, Gimpelman returned from Florida to find not only a young black usher tending the ticket stand of the Rococo but dozens of black patrons strutting about inside exchanging soul slaps.

Through auditorium doors he could hear raucous cheers and catcalls. In a disordered stride, he started toward the noise. "What the bloody shit's going on?"

The usher stopped him cold. "Where you think you're going, whitey?"

Praeger had hired the boy only the day before and hadn't as yet impressed upon him the niceties required by Kane Theatres. And now the boy would never get the chance to learn. Gimpelman fired him on the spot.

The boy stomped out, wadding his red jacket and throwing it into a vestibule butt can, at the same time swearing he was going straight to the offices of the NAACP, the Human Relations Commission, and the Black Panthers, among others.

As Gimpelman's blood pressure went up, his face took on the fiery glow of Yosemite Sam. "Where's that Winkle!"

Going no more than five paces he was approached by a hulking black patron in workshirt and muddy shoes. The man's eyes scanned Gimpelman up and down, knowing a boss when they saw one. "Fine motherfucking theatre, man," he said.

SUPERDUDE DAY

The call reached the censor board offices during the thread-up break between the latest Robert Redford and the morning porno. Attorney General Tassone and his lackey had just arrived. The anonymous voice informed them that Vita Vibes was doing her thing in *Mondo Sucko* on screen at the Rococo.

Tassone's countenance brightened considerably when he heard the news. He had been out of town the week the censor board possessed a print of *Mondo Sucko* and had missed the screenings—all seventeen of them. Quickly, he cloaked his glee with indignant and officious concern. He suggested they all use his siren-equipped state car and proceed to Stricker Street forthwith.

The Three Stooges went for their coats.

While making inspection rounds Praeger began noticing graffiti on the walls of the men's room, eye level, above the urinals: *Crockett eats shit. Eat my shit.*

He left a note for Dewey to remove them. Next day they were gone.

Then, two days later, others appeared. *Fuck you Crockett. Eat my ass Crockett.* Praeger left another note. Again, they were scrubbed away.

Soon afterward, though, he discovered others, larger, written with red Magic Marker inside the four toilet stalls of the ladies' room. *Crockett sucks. Suck my juicy cock Crockett.*

Praeger got the number of the cleaning service from his file and dialed on the pay phone.

"This is Praeger at the Rococo, Mr. Crockett. Think I better have a word with you about Dewey."

Lebowitz thought up a grand scheme.

He began charging an extra nickel on every popcorn box and soda cup. He posted a sign telling the people it was a "deposit." They would get the nickel back, the sign explained, when they returned the empty container.

Within a day, all four downtown theatres had implemented the brain storm. He justified himself with Gimpelman by pointing out the money it would save—money normally spent for janitorial personnel. Even with the increased patronage, he argued, it would keep the theatres tidy, foregoing the need to pay Crockett to bring in extra help.

Gimpelman acquiesced.

Of course, as Lebowitz knew, and as he failed to mention, most people would just throw the cups away. Who was going to hack the concession line for five cents?

All he had to do was have his girls keep the deposit money separate and he would be a nickel richer after each sale.

Nickels added up.

SUPERDUDE DAY

Herman Kane, with aid of walking stick, waddled the three blocks to the Rococo. When he came within earshot and heard the ripple of chanting blacks surrounding the building, he turned in his tracks and began to waddle the three blocks back to his office.

Crossing Simone Avenue he heard a siren. Looking about for a fire engine, he was all but run down by an official-appearing vehicle full of crazy-eyed people. The car skidded against the curb and came to a halt, where it sat for a moment, siren fading, rocking on its Michelins.

Suddenly, a head popped from the driver's window. Herman Kane raised his walking stick. He was about to swing when he recognized the attorney general of the state—a man with whom he'd once shared a business venture, a now-defunct travel agency known as T-K Tours, Inc.

Years earlier, somewhere in the Pyrenees, a T-K tour of Gobelin tapestry exhibits had gotten stranded, fundless, finding themselves subject to the charity of local villagers. It took two months for Kane and Tassone to get the group stateside. But even more mortifying, three members stayed on—one marrying the town butcher, one taking a teaching position at the local *lycée,* and one, a

165

young man of draft age, dropping from sight completely, never to be heard from again.

T-K Tours filed under Chapter Thirteen shortly thereafter.

"Herman, Herman . . . what are you doing to us with this thing at the Rococo?" cried Tassone. "You know we can't let you get away with stuff like that—"

"You still got your driver's license, Louis?"

"—that filth!"

"Filth? What filth? *Superdude* ain't filth. Maybe crap —but it's rated and censored crap. And you can't touch it."

"Don't play dumb. I mean *Mondo Sucko*."

"*What?*"

"*Mondo Sucko's* on the screen at the Rococo, right this minute."

Herman Kane found himself speechless for a moment. "Better you should have run over me," he said finally.

"Jump in, Herman. We've got to get to the bottom of this."

Crockett fired Dewey, who in turn went out in a profane blaze of glory with a purple Magic Marker. Praeger spent the next few days staying after the last show to gather the trash and swab the toilets. A replacement had yet to be sent for Dewey. No one at the cleaning service wanted anything to do with the place. Crockett was holding out, citing the extra work involved, trying to negotiate a new contract. Gimpelman didn't want to hear it.

Gimpelman figured the janitorial services were a waste anyhow. Lebowitz's new plan would take care of it. Who needed them. He fired them.

Gimpelman was adept at juggling accounts. At skimming by with minimal resources. At keeping the old man happy. He was also adept at handling creditors. "If my mother could carry me for nine months," he often told them, "you can fucking-well carry me for ninety days. . . ."

Six months earlier, hopelessly behind in premium payments, he had been forced to let the chain's insurance lapse. So nasty was the severance that Kane Theatres found itself nonrenewable, blacklisted. No agency in town would touch them. Now, with money pouring through the box office, Gimpelman began to fret about holdups.

He remembered screening a film recently where a loner of a cop toted about a .44 magnum revolver. It had impressed him no end. At an expense of $260 apiece he ordered one each for the downtown theatres—to be kept in the money boxes along with a carton of fifty cartridges.

The implication was not lost on the managers: they were to protect the receipts of Kane Theatres to the last bullet.

A .44 magnum was, in actuality, the most absurd weapon to drop in the lap of a novice. Its impact could make powder of a cinder block. Recoil was so great that firing it rapidly was impossible. Aiming the monster was a joke. Misplaced shots could penetrate walls and ceilings, could chart a lethal path for a half mile.

All of this making it just the weapon Gimpelman wanted; its psychological mystique was legend in the street. He made sure word leaked out that the revered pieces were at hand.

Within a week both the Eagle and Belvedere had their safes cracked. Besides the cash banks and trays of miscellaneous coinage, the .44 magnums and cartridges were taken.

Lebowitz's concession scheme began to work not so well.

Clans of street urchins took up roving from theatre to theatre, breaking down exit doors, maneuvering through the aisles, stepping over patrons, moving spiderlike on hands and knees by the dozens, filling plastic trash bags with refundable cups and boxes.

Lebowitz confronted a trio of them in the lobby of the

Eagle. He tried to argue them out of the huge refund due
on the load they were hauling. It didn't work. He got a
cut lip and a hundred and thirty-five dollar sport coat
ripped for his trouble.

The kids were no dummies, even up against Lebowitz.
After a batch was turned in and dispatched by an usher
to the padlocked dumpster, the same group would then
pry the container open and haul the cups to another
theatre—cashing them in again.

Within a week the whole of downtown was full of
marauding gangs toting plastic sacks over their shoulders
like an army of pickaninny Santas, going Eagle to Granada, Belvedere to Rococo, scattering nondeposit droppings along the way.

Each evening as the house lights came on Praeger
would make his final round among sticky rivers of upturned drinks, contraband pork bones, broken wine bottles, mustard-smeared seats, and mashed, half-devoured
frankfurters—but nary a cup or box.

He had been having Harry Harp do the best he could
between shows, shoveling the residue from aisles, mop-
ping the most hazardous puddles, scraping up chewing
gum.

But that, of course, was not enough.

Praeger went to see Gimpelman.

He maneuvered through the front office, among potted
plastic palms and cubicles of potato-chip-eating girls,
walking directly into the general manager's office.

Gimpelman was on the phone. "Look, sweetheart," he
was saying, "I appreciate what you're doing for us. I'm
coming to you hat in hand. But, look, we get an icy

night and take in twelve bucks in a unit that costs three
hundred a day to turn the key in the door. Who the fuck
are you kidding? Am I kidding you? You kidding me?
I haven't made the house nut in two months with your
stuff. . . ."

He listened for a moment, glancing up at Praeger.

"Yeah, yeah," he went on, "you want me to keep prod-
uct so you'll look good in New York—well, you've got
maybe fifty units to play with. You can spread grosses.
That doesn't help me and my four walls, sweetheart.
We're dying here. People just won't swallow some of this
shit. This is a hard money town, my friend. They want
championship football, baseball, basketball, *and* hockey.
And it's the same story with movies. Give me some good
fast action on the screen, some black action for downtown
—not these twelve-million-dollar dogs you're puking out."

He cupped his hand over the mouthpiece, mimicking
the party on the other end. "What the fuck do you want,
Praeger?" he hissed.

"A cleaning service."

"Shit! Shit!" yelled Gimpelman back into the phone.
"A bush town? You think this is a bush town. Well, turds
on you then, that's what I say. It's a town where nobody's
fool enough to pay three dollars for five spears of aspar-
agus in a restaurant—or a shitty movie. That's what it is."

Again, Gimpelman cupped the receiver. "Forget it,"
he said.

"But—"

"*But*, my ass! Lebowitz solved the problem for you.
What are you complaining? If it's still dirty, leave it
dirty. The fucking savages won't know the difference."

As word of Lebowitz's folly spread, older gangs, more sophisticated in strong-arm methods, came in from the projects. They began waylaying the younger scavengers, taking their booty of refundables. Fights broke out. Gang pitted itself against gang. The newspapers printed a running account. Police intelligence became involved. Narcs were brought in; they thought they were cracking rival drug rings.

Lebowitz dropped the scheme after learning that the outlay of deposits exceeded intake—by seven hundred and fifty-four dollars.

Praeger opened on the next day Hawkes was off. It was his turn to work a double. As he unlocked the front doors he knew something was wrong. Then, stepping into the lobby, he realized what it was.

The Rococo was clean.

He walked to the auditorium entrance and yelled down over the rows of empty seats, "Mr. Max, you old bastard you, don't get into this! It's my theatre. My problem. Stay down there and cut up your newspapers! I won't have it, you hear!"

No answer came.

SUPERDUDE DAY

Three minutes remained of *Mondo Sucko*. Vita Vibes was on her last penis, going down the home stretch.

Descending the Grand Staircase, revolver tucked out of sight, Praeger began noticing young patrons wandering about pinning on buttons, holding them out for inspection, comparing them, laughing about them. *How's Your Firn?*

The Button Man! Something's happened to The Button Man.

Praeger grabbed the boy nearest him, shaking the pieces of tin from his hand. "Where is he?" he demanded.

The boy stood stock-still, bearing a frightful look.

"Where's the man with the buttons?"

A cloak of innocence spread over the boy's face, until Praeger pinched it away, stretching the skin as if the boy were made of rubber. "Where is he, I said!" The boy motioned toward the lobby soda machine. As Praeger turned to look, he jerked away and bounded up the Grand Staircase.

Beyond the railing, Praeger could see a crowd in the lobby. A sickly feeling churned through him as he began pushing his way toward it, crunching scattered buttons on the stairway.

God is Love.

173

Praeger began staying later into the night. He found himself polishing brass, scrubbing marble, repairing seats, dusting chandeliers.

Afterward, walking out into the deserted streets of blinking traffic lights and windswept trash, into the still chilling approach of dawn, he experienced each time a shivering sense of accomplishment worth every moment —an almost perverse enjoyment of what he was doing.

Harry Harp returned to the Rococo one night after closing. He had forgotten some groceries left cooling in the ice maker. He peered through the front doors before pounding and caught Praeger vacuuming the lobby. Praeger opened the door for him. Harry Harp got his shopping bag and left. He didn't say anything.

Much to his credit, considering his perpetual motion, Teddy Winkle noticed the improved appearance of the Rococo. He mentioned it to Praeger. Praeger just shrugged it off.

Winkle said no more. He was wise enough to let it lie. Besides, he had plenty on his mind.

Rumor had a ticket racket flourishing at the Eagle. A

174

doorman was palming tickets and a cashier was reselling them. Wanting eyewitness proof before acting, Teddy Winkle was spending most of his time perched with binoculars on a ledge of the Parkarama Parkade across the street from the Eagle.

Second day out his surveillance ended. He fell off the ledge and broke some things, including a leg, when he landed in the Parkarama entranceway two levels below.

Two nights after Harry Harp had seen Praeger cleaning the Rococo, he and Brother Jason hung around the lobby after closing.

"We's gonna help," said Brother Jason.

"Don't be ridiculous."

"I ain't got nowhere to go," said Harry Harp. "Except maybe the barroom up the street or maybe sit in my room and listen to Perry Peck on the all-night talk show. . . ."

"Yeah, me either," said Brother Jason. "Besides, I'm like you. Never did like working around filth—even if it ain't mine."

Praeger said nothing. He walked away, coming back shortly with two straw brooms and a handful of trash bags.

SUPERDUDE DAY

Superdude, using a screwdriver found in Teddy Winkle's desk drawer, took the hinges off the door, pulling it open enough to squeeze out.

A roaring fistfight was in progress on the upper concourse between a rotund dwarf in pimp rags and his companion, a six-foot transvestite in a Korean fright wig.

"My money on the queen," exclaimed a gleeful voice, bumping past Superdude.

Superdude saw his chance. No one was paying him any attention. He pulled his cape up around his nose and edged toward the darkness of the balcony. Just as he entered, the house lights began to brighten. *Mondo Sucko* was ending.

Backing off, he flung some curtains aside and, seeking escape, kicked open a black door. Without knowing it, he was entering the secret domain of Praeger—and Mr. Max.

Teddy Winkle, out of the hospital and on crutches, returned to work, dragging himself about the spick-and-span lobby of the Rococo like Crabman in the comic books.

So impressed was he with the face lifting he even risked bringing Uncle Hermie around to inspect. The old man, cigar in mouth, walking stick at hand, got as far as the Grand Staircase before capitulating to fatigue. Someone rolled a chair out, into which he promptly lowered himself and sat for a half hour reminiscing on the building's showplace days—the days before it fell under his control.

Praeger, when questioned, remained vague about the refurbishing.

Teddy Winkle did most of the talking. Herman Kane smiled often, ending his stay by telling a few archaic jokes, departing with a firm handshake and optimism about chances for a successful year.

Hobbling on crutches, escorting his uncle, Winkle looked back when he reached the front entrance and crossed his eyes, glowing under a moronic grin—a high sign to Praeger.

All had gone well.

177

Lebowitz, hovering about like a latter-day Rasputin, for some reason had been excluded from the conversation, even ignored. Now, alone with Praeger, he stalked the carpet and scowled. "Relieve my girl for a break, Cliffie. I've got things to do."

Praeger merely looked at him.

"Just give her a break," he went on. "That's all I ask." His head tinged purple; it appeared oddly out of proportion. "You too damn good for that? I've got business to take care of, you know. I've got the rest of my stands to look after."

"So go look after them."

"What's that suppose to mean?"

Praeger started away, without answering.

Lebowitz grabbed his arm. "Look, pal, Daddy Kane pays his managers with concession profits. You know. So you figure it out. Whether you guessed it or not, your salary comes from me." Breathing erratically, he released his grip and forced a smile of benevolence. "Believe me, Cliffie, it comes from me."

"How about a raise then?"

"Look, so what's with the big deal? All I ask is twenty minutes. I need help. There're lines over at the Eagle. You don't know the business I'm losing with that molasses ass over there. You don't know. . . ."

"Mr. Lebowitz, the Eagle hasn't had a line since *Gone with the Wind*."

"God give me hemorrhoids if I'm lying. Black action's packing them in. All niggers. What do you think resurrected Daddy Kane? Downtown's turning a profit for a change."

Praeger waved him away. "So hire some more help."

"What about now? Like you never heard of an emergency? Never heard of giving a hand?" He paused, heaving. "I know what it is. Don't think I don't. You're pissed-off because of Wanda."

"What?"

"Guess you heard those lies she told on me."

Praeger studied with more care than usual the egg-shaped figure standing before him—seeing an expression of vulnerability he would have thought not possible.

"Well, I didn't touch her. I don't care what she told her mother. Or Daddy Kane. I didn't touch her. I only gave her a ride home." His arms suddenly dropped at his side. "What do I want with a little nigger girl? Some thanks I get for being decent to these bitches."

Praeger said nothing.

"Just do me this one favor, huh?" said Lebowitz, finally, his balloon jowls swelling.

"Forget it."

"What about Christmas, Cliffie baby? I'll remember you next Christmas. You know what I mean?"

"I think I can live without your box of candy."

"So I had a bad year. You know that. Why throw that up in my face?"

"Get out of here, Mr. Lebowitz."

"*Huh?*"

"Get the fuck out of my theatre."

"Who you think you're talking to?"

Praeger looked him up and down. "A big fat shyster crook," he said.

A milky glaze seemed to cover Lebowitz's eyes. "*Crook!* I'm a crook because I'm trying to earn a buck? What d'you know? What d'you think it takes to send my kids to college? Or pay doctor bills? I've got a heart condition. You didn't know that, did you?"

"You're still a crook."

"A man's got to make out best he can these days. Believe me, Cliffie, you'll see when you get older. Making a buck is all that matters. Making it now, now."

Praeger felt his fingers digging into his palms.

"The buck is *everything*. The almighty buck. Maybe good health is all right. You know. But doctors can be bought. . . ."

"You're sick, man."

Lebowitz recoiled. "Don't tell me about being sick, you shit. You're so fucked up your asshole talks." He made an elaborate display of tapping his temples, backing away in case Praeger took a swing. "I've watched you. Staring at the wall. Goddamn eyeballs rolling around. Going backstage all the time. Staying after closing."

"That's my problem."

"You're not getting paid for *problems*."

Praeger wheeled toward the office door, stepping quickly, adrenal fluids raging within his body. When he reappeared, holding a freshly swollen fist and leaving a new dent in his filing cabinet Benny Lebowitz was gone.

Teddy Winkle returned. He hobbled aimlessly about the lobby for a few minutes before gathering nerve enough to stick his head through the office doorway. "Uh, I been meaning to ask you, Cliff. Uh, like how's all of this getting done?"

"Staff's doing it."

"*What!*" A mask of terror immediately slid over his face, the rest of his body disintegrated into a waiting chair. "Whose payroll they doing it on? Jesus. What if Gimpelman finds out? Oh, sweet Jesus!"

"They're just doing it, that's all."

"Huh . . . ?"

"Nothing's on anybody's payroll."

"*Huh?*"

"Don't worry about it."

"They *stupid* or something?"

"I guess."

"Jesus," said Teddy Winkle.

50

SUPERDUDE DAY

In the crevice between the soda machine and the auditorium wall, Praeger found The Button Man. Teen-agers were crowded around the carcass, picking and pawing. Praeger pushed his way through, yelling aloud, flinging bodies against the wall.

"The man crazy! He crazy!"

A few youngsters remained to challenge him. But the sight of the drawn revolver kept them at a distance.

"You fools, I told you he was crazy!"

The Button Man's head lay to one side. He was in a sitting position, unconscious against the wall. Most of his clothing had been ripped away with the buttons, down to ugly froglike flesh and stained, gray undergarments.

Praeger waved his revolver at the crowd. "Back away or I'm going to start killing people. I swear it. I swear it. . . ."

51

"I don't understand it." Michele was sitting on the couch, her animals gathered around, when he walked in. "I just don't understand it, Praeger," she said. She had waited up for him. It was almost dawn. "I don't understand what's going down between us anymore. Where do you go every night?"

Praeger took his coat off and hung it up. "You know I stay at the theatre."

"No, no, I don't know. I can't believe that anymore. Look, please, if it's another woman, just tell me, just be honest and say so, just *bloody* tell me. . . ."

"Nothing like that," mumbled Praeger, his eyes drooping with weariness.

"What's happening to you?" she cried. "You never come home. You're away every night. And when you are here, you're really not here either—your mind's somewhere else, not with me. I can't take it anymore, Praeger. Please, don't you understand?"

Praeger shrugged. "I'm just trying to clean up the Rococo."

"*Fuck the Rococo!*" she yelled, beginning to sob. "They're just using you, that's all. You're being a fool. You let people walk all over you. That sucking Kane organization's got you wrapped up namby-pamby in a neat little package. And after what happened to me, too. It's sick. I wouldn't set foot in the Rococo—but they've got you cowed into cleaning the place. And for nothing. You even told me you spend your own money for supplies—"

"You spend your own money on Baldy."

"Baldy's a living, breathing creature. The Rococo's nothing but a pile of brick put together with shit. Don't even compare them, Praeger. Don't you dare. . . ."

"That's not what I meant. It's hard to explain."

"You don't have to explain. You just don't have guts enough to stand up to them."

"It's got nothing to do with *them*."

"Then what? Who?" Tears began edging down her cheeks. "Who does it have to do with?"

"Michele, please, you're crying. . . ."

"I know I'm crying, Goddamnit. I can't help it. What's happening between us? Please tell me, somebody tell me. . . ."

Next morning a UPI truck delivered three crates of promotional items for what Gimpelman was calling Superdude Day. The crates contained Superdude pens and posters, balloons and buttons, T-shirts and trinkets.

Gimpelman had brainstormed the idea of having an old-fashioned première. He had screened a film in New York and, learning that the distributor was dropping it on the market without promotion, he smelled a sleeper. It was just garbage enough to go over at the Rococo. Crudely made, fast-paced black action, about a drug war in Harlem with a pimp-dealer for a hero.

The name of the film was *Superdude*.

Gimpelman knew he could pick it up at good terms; he also knew there was a possibility that its star would be available for a stage appearance.

Teddy Winkle, finally discovering from an usher what was going on, ricocheted about the lobby suffering mild hysteria. "Everybody's gotta wear a Superdude T-shirt, everybody, cashiers, everybody!"

"Who the hell's Superdude?" stammered Hawkes, trying to keep pace.

"Superdude's the baddest dude of all."

"Yeah—but like, who is he?"

"Some clown out of New York. Who cares. You know. Just so we do box office. It's gonna be like the thirties. The Rococo's gonna shine. And these Mau Mau's gonna love it. They gonna eat it up. Gobble. Gobble."

In a press release issued through the publicity department of Kane Theatres, it was announced that the Rococo Theatre on Stricker Street would henceforth be known as the Black Rococo.

Soul stations on the radio began to spout out a garbled, incoherent commercial spot—though apparently understood, for dozens of calls began pouring in about tickets and show times.

Hey, baby, man, you cool rockers out there. . . . Superdude flick coming I tell you. . . . Black Rococo, baby . . . you dig. . . . Gonna happen on April ninth, so get down there and rip those mothers off. . . . Low, low ticket prices . . . Superdude, yes, m'man, listen good, I said it, Superdude. He's the man who pushes, he's the man who pimps, he's the MAN!

With Superdude Day fast approaching, Teddy Winkle started an incessant chant: "I'm going out of my mind, I'm going out of my mind!" He traded his latest Mickey Mouse T-shirt for a Superdude T-shirt and began flashing it indiscriminately.

Other than the night he was locked up, Teddy Winkle hadn't been in such a tether since what was known as the Great Blondie Fiasco of a year earlier.

The Great Blondie Fiasco was vintage Winklese.

Upon becoming district manager, his fetish for blondes had caused him to hire all who applied. He would then set out on a course of seduction. Soon, he had so many cashiers working downtown that the managers could only schedule each a day or two a week. And so many looked identical that paychecks were always getting mixed up— not to mention other embarrassments, such as Teddy Winkle getting them mixed up. Those in various stages of seduction became indignant; they wanted more hours and longer breaks. Confusion reigned. After a while he didn't know which ones he was doing what with and which ones he was not doing what with. He had a nervous breakdown of sorts. The accounting office eventually issued a bundle of bonus checks to appease those threatening lawsuits or worse, following which Herman Kane personally pruned the harem within manageable bounds.

"I'm going out of my mind! I'm going out of my mind!"

Lebowitz remained the skeptic. Superdude Day could easily be a disaster. The film could turn out to be a hunk of shit, which he openly suspected.

He was hesitant to stock a heavy inventory. Being stuck with leftover perishables wasn't his style: hard as he tried, no one was much interested in three-day-old hot dogs.

They tended to shrivel up and take on odd hues.

With little more than a week to go Gimpelman settled upon his promotional scheme for the première. A rush order produced ten thousand flyers which were dumped on Teddy Winkle to be distributed in the black neighborhoods.

Teddy Winkle, in turn, dumped them on the downtown managers. The downtown managers dumped them on the ushers. The ushers dumped them into gutters.

Yet, despite all of this, gusts of March wind saw to their distribution.

KANE THEATRES FIGHTS INFLATION

Superdude Day—*The Black Rococo Theatre*—April 9
Good Friday—No School

GIANT ALL-DAY EXCITEMENT SPECTACULAR
Special Première Engagement

SUPERDUDE

Doors Open 9:00 A.M.

1st one hundred patrons   Admission only 25 cents
2nd one hundred patrons   Admission only 50 cents
3rd one hundred patrons   Admission only 75 cents
4th one hundred patrons   Admission only one dollar

All Thereafter $1.25

Colossal Black Action Hit—Tell Your Brothers
Biggest Soul Spectacular Ever!!!!

52

SUPERDUDE DAY

Praeger put The Button Man over his shoulders and zig-zagged through the crowd, lugging him up the Grand Staircase to Winkle's office. He found the door off its hinges and Superdude gone.

He lowered the weight from his back and picked up the phone. It was dead.

In the auditorium, with house lights illuminating the audience, impatient chants began to rise from the seats, echoing to the building's dome. Different this time, everyone sensed. The tremolo more ominous, rising amain.

Praeger ignored them. It was all lost on him for the moment. His mind was charged with reaching a phone.

Ambulances had to be brought in. The Button Man was lying crumpled on Winkle's floor. The people outside in the street had to know what was going on. The authorities had to know. Someone had to come in and put an end to it.

It's become all madness, he mumbled, striking out again for the lower level.

The pay station in the lobby was his next hope—but reaching it, he found the equipment ripped from its mountings, the change box pried open.

Then he heard a horrid sound.

A skin-rippling scream came from the ladies' room. He struggled past the queue of waiting, tight-lipped women and pushed through the door. The smell was nauseating. He held his nose, gagging. At the far end a figure was cowering under a washbasin. Teen-age girls with braided, beribboned hair were dancing about it, squealing, throwing cups of water. The figure scratched out, then hunched further into the crevice. Its clothing was sopping. It was blubbering hysterically, clutching an orange life preserver. . . .

It was The Umbrella Lady.

Praeger elbowed the girls away, making an opening. The Umbrella Lady sprang forward, growling and yapping like a trapped animal, her eyes insane as she careened aside a vanity, tumbling chairs in her path out the door.

He tried to go after her. But it was hopeless. A dozen hands began slapping at him, attempting to stop him, trying to ask questions, wanting money back, wanting Superdude, wanting to know where the exits were, wanting to know how to reach the street.

Faces began swirling about him. Making him dizzy. Voiceless mouths opened, barking at him. Rotting teeth grinned perverse fleers. Bleary, accusing eyes stabbed his skin.

He reached the front entrance and paused amid the confusion. All-Stars were positioned with their clubs in riot stance, facing the mob outside, beyond the secured doors. Suddenly, everything was toned ugly and gray. Seeing him through the reflections in the glass at the bank of doors, a woman grotesque in countenance beneath a huge floppy hat began screaming: "There he is! There's that white motherfucking manager!"

Others began pounding on the doorframes and glass, being pressed from behind in a bone-crushing surge.

Brother Jason appeared, tugging on his coat sleeve. Praeger jerked his arm away. He stared at the doorman. Uncomprehending. The old man's clothes were disheveled; his face was swathed with tiny beads of sweat. "People's tired of waiting for Superdude, Mr. Praeger. They's down front trying to get out—but the exits is chained up."

Praeger turned away. He hunched his shoulders forward as if to form a cocoon. But he found neither comfort nor salvation. His whole life was flip-flopping past in comic book sequence, with spoken parts entrapped in balloons—the hieroglyphics of his day—and he was helpless to control it. He edged against the ticket stand. He could feel himself shivering. He wrapped his arms about his chest.

"They's chained, Mr. Praeger. Don't you hear, they's chained."

All at once, the groan of twisting metal filled the vestibule. Praeger spun in time to witness a brace of doors buckle and pop. The frames twisted, forming pretzels. Glass shattered. Scores of people jammed the opening. Blood angry. Most had been waiting hours. Women with youngsters stumbled forward, whooping, falling to their knees, clawing for space; couples cleaved together and pushed as one; sulky-eyed boys leapt past them all, darting like thieves, mingling inside.

Praeger started for his office. He had to get the exit keys. He had to unchain the alley doors.

Bodies swept past him. All at once he felt a sharp pain. Something was biting his leg. He kicked by reflex. His foot struck the face of an enraged woman, bloodying her nose, knocking her floppy hat askew. All-Stars rushed forward to assist at the entrance, sneering and huffing. Gold teeth glistened as they pounded with their billies. People caught in the vice tried to scramble out, shielding their heads—but it was hopeless.

The furthermost door gave with a loud snap. The initial wave ploughed through under its own inertia. Then, behind, came gangs of street thugs, slithering like reptiles, weaving frantically by dozens toward the rear of the lobby, dissipating beyond the concession stand.

Praeger reeled, swept aside by the flood and tumult. Torsos and limbs filled the gap he left, rushing in around him, bumping him, racking him, jabbing him. . . .

God! God! I've got to get to the keys!

53

"Baldy's dead," said Michele.

She was standing at the door. Her face was impassive. Every light in the apartment was on, glaring. Praeger, again, had stayed late at the Rococo.

"*Dead?*" he said. He shivered. Outside it was storming. He was soaked.

"I had him put to sleep."

He looked at her. He had a feeling he had lived it all before.

"I needed you, Praeger. You don't know what I've been through."

"I'm sorry."

She moved out of his way. "Too late," she mumbled. "It's too late."

"What are you talking about? What happened with Baldy?"

"He's been alone all these months. Stuffed in that little cage."

"You knew that."

She was quiet for a moment. "The vet called. . . ." All at once her voice trailed off.

"And?"

"He said he wouldn't have the treatments on his con-

192

science anymore. He refused to continue. He was really upset. I just hadn't realized it was so bad. . . ."

"What did you expect?"

"I didn't know it was hopeless. I didn't know Baldy's kidneys were being eaten away by the arsenic. The vet said he should have been put to sleep months ago. He suffered every minute." She paused and wiped the hair away from her face. "I told him to take Baldy out in the sunshine for a few minutes . . . before he did it. Except the sun wasn't shining. Poor Baldy. . . ."

Praeger said nothing.

"So it's done," she said.

Cardboard boxes were scattered about the room; curtains were down. "Why are your things packed?" he asked.

"I'm leaving."

He felt his chest contract, then swell; lumps of mucus drained into his throat until he could barely breathe.

"You were right, Praeger, you bastard. You were right all along by staying away from living things. It hurts too much, doesn't it? Your theatre, your precious Rococo, your fucking hunks of inanimate steel and brick are the answer, aren't they?" She began weeping. "Anything that doesn't draw a breath, or love, or feel. . . ."

He tried to put his arm around her, but she jerked away.

"I'll be by tomorrow for my things," she said, lips trembling. "I've taken Gomer and the rest away already."

"What are you going to do?"

She shrugged. "Try to make some sense of it all, I guess. Catch a ride north with my animals. Look for a new Walden. . . ."

"And what am I going to do?"

When she was gone, Praeger slumped to the floor. He sat there for a long time among the floating balls of animal fur, batting them about with his hand. He still had his raincoat on; puddles of water outlined his body on the carpet.

Outside the window a ribbon of orange appeared, beyond the storm clouds, glowing with the approach of dawn.

It was Superdude Day.

SUPERDUDE DAY

Tassone's state car had little trouble reaching the Rococo. Only a few gawkers, a few scattered knots of people, remained in the street. Most everyone had made it through the twisted doors—leaving a trail of coffee cups, potato chip bags, cigarette butts, and pimpmobile debris.

Old man Kane was first out, swinging his walking stick. "My God, what's happened here? *Police!* These people are going in *without tickets! Police!* Arrest everybody. Arrest them!"

"Now, Herman, calm down," said Tassone, opening his door. "I don't see any police. Save your breath. Let's take care of first things first, like *Mondo Sucko*."

"Shove *Mondo Sucko*! One of my theatres is being torn apart. What's going on? Where're the coppers?"

Tassone looked around. "They're gone," he said.

"Gone! What do you mean *gone*?"

The Three Stooges clambered out and stood on the sidewalk. Funnels of wind whirled paper and trash about them. "Gone where?" asked the bespectacled pharmacist-cum-censor with much concern, appearing intimidated and woebegone away from the sanctuary of the screening room.

"Police got orders to avoid racial confrontations," whispered Tassone, his tone implying that he was privy to all manner of secret stratagems. "They must have seen the potential here and withdrawn—"

"Potential!" screamed Herman Kane. "This ain't no potential here. This is a *real* catastrophe. Who's going to buy a ticket if they can just walk in? Would you? It's criminal what we got here."

"Uncle Hermie!" came a voice.

"Huh? Who said that?"

"Uncle Hermie!" The utterance was repeated, anxious, hesitant. It seemed to be coming from the theatre's façade, from the enclave of shattered glass and indented metal and burst light bulbs that was once the box office.

Herman Kane turned and squinted his eyes. Within the opening he saw an arm extend upward and, at counter level, a nose and pair of creepy eyes belonging to his nephew. "Pssssst! Pssssst! Uncle Hermie!" the voice pleaded in a low, whiny hiss.

The group moved closer, forming a semicircle.

Teddy Winkle and Hawkes were crouched together among upturned chairs and strewn paperwork on the box office floor. Nearby, Ida Schmidt sat smacking gum and reading a *True Romance* magazine. Her dress was ripped and her lipstick smeared.

"Oh, my goodness!" said one of the censor ladies.

Teddy Winkle peeped side to side, frowning, then pointed frantically at a bundle clutched against his chest. "I've got seventeen thousand three hundred and forty-six dollars in small bills here—and no way out!"

Old man Kane wet his lips.

"We tried to put it in the safe," chimed in Hawkes, "but—"

"But somebody broke into Praeger's office and rolled it out into the lobby, then into the men's room."

"Yeah, it's sitting there now," said Hawkes. His nose was swollen and discolored; he was having trouble speaking.

"Ida got shoved around, too," said Teddy Winkle.

Herman Kane stuck a hand through the opening. "Gimme the money, gimme the money."

"We'll take my car, Herman," said Tassone, stepping closer, whispering. "I'll get you back to your office—then it's *Mondo Sucko* for me."

"Gimme the money," said Herman Kane, "gimme the money."

"I'll find a bag," said Hawkes.

"Gimme the money!"

"Make two trips."

"Gimme it all, gimme it all!"

"Don't get too close."

"Gimme it."

"Watch out, Uncle Hermie, you're knocking against loose glass. . . ."

"Be careful, Herman!"

"Gimme."

"*Look out!*"

Herman Kane stumbled backward, ducking icicles of falling glass. Banknotes by the batches slid out of his grip and over his stomach. Yet, nary a one touched cement: a whirlwind caught them and spun them—a dirty-green cyclone—above everyone's head.

"*My God, my God!*"

"Look at it all go."

"Grab them, grab them quick!"

"Finders keepers," cried the blowzy censor lady, leaping skyward, snatching down fives and tens, "losers weepers. . . ."

55

SUPERDUDE DAY

Superdude found himself stumbling about backstage, groping through the darkness. Beyond the screen and undrawn curtain he could hear thousands of chattering voices.

Suddenly, near him, a motor began whining. The curtain spread apart with a jerk, then opened in a mechanical drone. Cascades of light struck the sceen. Music blared.

An old two-reeler, scratched and flickering, appeared: Ledbetter was getting desperate.

Able to see now, Superdude began turning doorknobs, seeking an escape. Each cubicle was locked or boarded—except one, the last he tried. Its door popped open with a single push.

Superdude was about to enter when he gave a start and froze. Someone's hand touched his elbow. . . .

SUPERDUDE DAY

As the last of the crashers plummeted past, Praeger made it to his office. The door was beaten in. The place was ransacked. Frantically, his fingers touched the hook above the pay phone. Gone! The exit keys were gone! He backed out of the doorway.

At once, he realized who had them.

He looked toward the concession stand. Something was smoking. He smelled burning rubber. Standing on tiptoes, he strained to see above the heads. Lebowitz was behind the stand, stripped to an undershirt, trying to beat out a fiery extension cord.

"Pull it from the wall!" Praeger yelled. "Pull it out!"

A concession girl heard him and kicked the plug free of the sparking receptacle, then poured orange drink on the cord.

Too late.

Bunting draped about the stand burst afire. A blaze hopscotched across greasy carpeting, leaping trash barrel to trash barrel, finally climbing to the ceiling.

It was out of control.

Clawing through the smoke, Praeger approached the side of the counter. "The exits are chained, the keys are gone," he gasped. "Who did it, Lebowitz?"

"I did!" cried the fat man, without looking. He was on hands and knees stuffing money into his pockets. "What the fuck's it to you. . . . ?"

Praeger drew his .44 magnum. He pointed it at the sweating forehead, waited until the eyes raised upward, then squeezed the trigger.

57

SUPERDUDE DAY

"Who is you?"

"I'm Mr. Max, sir. My family once owned this building—and I once ran it."

"You ain't no friend of that crazy manager I hopes."

"Clinton Clifton?"

"Somethin' like that."

"He's a good boy. He tries."

"Yeah—tries to kill me. . . ."

Mr. Max squeezed Superdude's arm in a gesture of camaraderie. "Tut-tut," he said.

"Which way to the street, man?"

"Going somewhere?"

"The cat wearing these rags is staying," said Superdude, shedding his full-length black cape and chinchilla hat, "but Lorenzo Jones is hauling ass back to Harlem."

"Sorry to hear that."

"Why you sorry?" he mumbled, frantically plucking rhinestones from his jersey.

"People out there paid a lot of money for a look at you. People that can ill-afford it."

"Those dudes want my bones!"

"Too bad," said Mr. Max. "Nothing like this has ever happened at the Rococo. Quite a pity it should begin now—"

"*Quite a pity . . . !*" Lorenzo was now ripping velveteen

202

material off both arms. "Look, m'man, you whiteys dressed me up in these pimp clothes and ran me around Harlem with a camera stuck up my ass, making me do jiveshit no black man ever heard of . . . then you bring me down here with half a city on a high, with the peoples thinking they's gonna pay dollars and see a real-life-ghetto-hero—well, *fuck your idea of a ghetto hero!* You honkies and your make-believe movies got nothing to do with the ghetto, got nothing to do with what us black peoples go through. . . ."

"I had nothing to do with it either, lad—"

"You're standing *here*, ain't you?" Lorenzo's pullover was shredded down to a funky T-shirt which—along with his shorts and socks—were the only trappings not supplied by Gimpelman. He wadded the material and threw it to the floor.

"So I am," said Mr. Max. He blinked his eyes, unseeing; his shoulders seemed to droop. "So I am."

"Yeah . . ." huffed Superdude.

Mr. Max straightened somewhat. "Why don't you tell the people, Lorenzo? Step out there and tell the audience what you've told me."

"I ain't being nobody's fool no more."

"Someone's got to do it." Mr. Max pushed the heavy curtain aside. He walked onstage. "Come on, Lorenzo, they'll never believe me. . . ."

Superdude, immovable as Gibraltar, gave him the finger.

Minutes earlier, after smelling smoke, Ledbetter had cut the film in midframe, put a spot center stage, and abandoned the booth with his dailies.

Mr. Max stepped into the lone light.

"Ladies and gentlemen, my name is John Maximillian. Lot of people once called me Mr. Max—back in the days when I used this stage to introduce vaudeville acts." The audience stirred; Superdude this man wasn't. "It's been a long time between acts, believe me. But here I am. And I want to personally welcome you to the Rococo—Showplace of the East."

"You're supposed to be dead!" someone yelled.

Mr. Max smiled. "A misunderstanding, I assure you. Years ago, the hotel I lived in burned to the ground. My bill with them was considerable. I just never returned to pay it."

The audience laughed.

"After reading my own obituary—which I thought rather nice—I just let things lie. . . ."

"Where's Superdude?" called out several people. "We wants Superdude."

"He's here, I assure you. Waiting offstage this very moment—"

"We's heard *that* before."

Mr. Max stepped forward, onto the proscenium. The audience became still. His cheeks flushed before them; his teeth glittered in the spotlight. "Ladies and gentlemen, here he is—as the Rococo Theatre promised—the man you've been patiently awaiting." He turned, brimming with confidence, and motioned toward the wings. "Superdude, *in person!*"

SUPERDUDE DAY

The bullet severed the top of Lebowitz's head. He rolled backward, eyes still open, thrashing his arms. Then he pitched forward against the deep fryers, tipping them over.

Scalding grease inundated his body, splattering the flaming walls and cabinets.

Concession girls squealed and jumped aside.

Praeger leapt the counter. He tossed the revolver away and began digging into Lebowitz's clothing. Grease seared the hair from his hands. His lungs began filling with smoke.

At last he found the keys. Buried in a pants pocket. He clutched them tightly and kicked open the concession door, shoving the girls out. Then he ran for the Grand Staircase.

He reached the upper concourse and looked over the railing. Muted, hysterical screams filtered up from below. The lobby was quickly emptying into Stricker Street. At the concession stand, beneath frying, charred comestibles—some sputtering and igniting into fiery missiles—Lebowitz's carcass lay on the floor, steaming.

Praeger pushed his way to the balcony entrance. The hallways were quiet. Untouched by smoke or confusion.

He entered, stumbling through aisles until he reached the uppermost exit. On screen, in black and white—with chauvinistic music and banners aflutter—a crew-cut zombie, swagger stick in hand, was speaking in a clipped voice.

It was the Marine Corps training film.

Using the keys, Praeger removed the padlock and chain holding the exit. Then he pushed the door ajar. Sunlight streamed across the front of the auditorium. Wind gusted through the opening. The audience glared upward, squinting and hooting. . . .

An escape was waiting, he knew. He could be away and free. Michele was still in the city. She hadn't left yet. He could find her and make things right. They could go into the mountains together, with the animals—into Canada if they had to—and never be found, never again speak of rape or draw a breath of lethal fume.

It was there—if he wanted salvation.

He closed the door. From the inside. Leaving it unchained. Then he went through the balcony to the next, and the next, until he was at the last. He stood outside for a moment on its metal landing, catching his breath, again tempted to flee.

Yet knowing the auditorium exits remained.

Suddenly, two men appeared. "Keep them doors shut, asshole!" said one.

"Where's Superdude, man?" The other, less diplomatic, grabbed Praeger's throat. "We're tired of—"

Praeger swung. Keys sailed. "Oh, fuck . . ." he moaned, watching them clang to the alley below. The first man cocked his fist, but Praeger bulled past. . . .

"You better run!"

Again inside, he maneuvered along the west wall, vanishing behind heavy curtain. The black door—his secret passage—was hanging open. He careened through, skipping down the stairway, coming out backstage.

Earth-shattering explosions peppered the screen; the roar of amplifiers caused the stage to tremble.

He knocked open an abandoned maintenance room. Cobwebs and stalactites of dust hung at face level. The light switch didn't work. He entered, hands held as shields, stumbling sightless among piles of trash, sandbags, cans of dried lacquer, shovels, sawhorses. In a dim corner he rummaged through an assortment of hammers, finally choosing a sledge.

It was quiet when he emerged.

The film had ended. He could see the diffused glare of a spotlight on stage. Someone was talking to the audience. It was Mr. Max, he realized. The old man was rambling on about not returning to his hotel after a fire, about reading his own obituary. . . .

I should have known, thought Praeger.

Then he caught sight of Superdude looming in the wings. "Still haven't paid dues, have you?" he whispered, approaching with the sledgehammer.

"Oh, Lawd!" the man cried, flailing through curtains, running on stage.

Praeger gave a token chase before jumping down among the audience. Hundreds of faces were canted toward the stage; Superdude was getting a standing ovation. Mr. Max was next to him, beaming, arms outstretched.

A faint, almost unnoticeable ribbon of smoke hung on the auditorium dome. Praeger ducked into the nearest exitway. At the door he raised the sledgehammer above his head and crashed down on the padlock and chain. The metal push bars collapsed. The door sprang open.

"What you doing, fool?" came a voice.

Praeger flattened against the wall. He could hear the jangle of paraphernalia. He could see the silhouette of an All-Star rushing him. Before he could fend him off, the man cracked down with a billy club.

Cringing, Praeger felt his shoulder cave in; he slumped forward, dazed. He tried to speak. Feeble rasping sounds came out of his mouth.

"Freeze," the security guard ordered, reaching for handcuffs.

Praeger lunged with the sledgehammer, striking low. Bone splintered. The All-Star tumbled backward, grappling with his holster. Praeger broke for the audience. He attempted to cross the footlights, but scores of awe-stricken people, crowding every inch, blocked his path.

Above him, Lorenzo Jones a.k.a. Superdude was springing about the stage on an invisible pogo stick. "Super-dude sucks!" he was yelling. "He ain't nothing but jive. Ain't nothing but a honky in blackface ripping you off. . . ."

Praeger climbed to the proscenium and lumbered across its breadth, holding his shoulder, trailing the sledgehammer; seeing him, Lorenzo panicked and ran in the opposite direction.

In the rear, flames had suddenly sprouted, lapping through the auditorium doorways. The entire lobby was ablaze.

People began bounding from their seats, into the aisles. Mr. Max remained alone in the spotlight. He was waving his arms, trying to calm the audience—then, with smooth, concise gestures, he began pointing out escape routes.

Praeger entered a hallway, going for another blocked exit. He was off-balance. Yet he struck with all the force he could gather—a single swipe of hammer which crashed through the push bars. But the chain held. He raised his arms again. His wrecked shoulder throbbed. He swung. The sledgehammer hit squarely, but the recoil pitched it backward, catching his leg, shattering the kneecap. He cried in pain. He clawed at the walls, trying to stay upright.

What a fuckup.

The door caught the wind and swung open. He tried to backtrack. Side exits still remained chained. Reaching them seemed hopeless. He was all but paralyzed. As if in a slow-motion sequence of film, he slid to the floor, crawling toward the auditorium, hearing the thunder of footfalls enter the hallway, rushing him, stampeding. . . .

Indeed.

59

SUPERDUDE DAY

Sirens wailed in the distance. People, tumbling over one another, were spewing from every exit, clambering down metal stairways aside the building. Smoke billowed a hundred meters into the air.

Superdude was among the first to reach the street. A swirl of paper money met him, slapping at his face, clinging to clothing, fluttering about his ankles. The sky was full of it. He tried to stop. But it was no good. The phalanx behind all but bulldozed him into the cement.

He kept running.

The façade of the Rococo was scorched black. Windows burst from their frames in fiery explosions. Hunks of blistered wood sailed in the air. The marquee on Stricker Street was blazing. Plastic letters heralding *Superdude* curled and popped to the sidewalk, bouncing and crackling, alighting random banknotes.

Superdude skipped through the volcanic shower.

Passing beneath the marquee, without breaking stride, he scooped up a handful of smoldering bills and ran helter-skelter for the Greyhound bus station.

SUPERDUDE DAY

"Exit left and right! Walk, please, ladies and gentlemen! Keep order!" Mr. Max—a spectral figure in smoke-shrouded light—was directing the evacuation from the proscenium. "Exit left and right!"

In front of him, edging along the orchestra seats, he spotted Praeger. The man was tattered and dazed, being jostled from all sides.

"Up here, lad!" Mr. Max called.

Praeger looked up, then reeled toward him. "The exits . . . exits . . ." he kept repeating.

"They're all open, lad." Mr. Max reached over the apron and steadied him, then began assisting him in a climb upward. "They've been battered open."

The smoke turned inky-thick. Curtains were roaring, afire on both sides of the stage. Above them, flaming debris began tumbling from the proscenium arch.

"This way!" cried Mr. Max. "It's our only hope!" He took Praeger's dangling arm and began pulling him in tow, kicking an opening through the screen.

They emerged by the dressing rooms, Praeger limping. Smoke billowed about them. They could barely breathe. Mr. Max continued to lead. He pulled Praeger into his makeshift office, slamming the door to preserve a pocket of oxygen.

On the desk, pages of an open pressbook were curling under the heat.

"Get out while you can. . . ." Mr. Max mumbled, voice trailing. He paused and glared up into Praeger's face. "Never look back . . . let them think you're dead. . . ."

Praeger was speechless.

Mr. Max entered a small closet and, shoving old costumes aside, unlatched a metal door.

Million Max's secreted passageway.

"Leave the city, lad," he coughed, ushering Praeger through the opening. "It's all become lunacy and pandering. . . ."

Suddenly the door clicked shut. Leaving Praeger in the alley.

"Mr. Max, *don't* . . ." He pounded on the metal surface. It was scorching hot. He pulled his hand away, flapping it in the air.

Down the alley, a hook-and-ladder was wheeling in from Stricker Street. It missed the turn. It had to brake and back up. There was much grinding of gears, much noise and confusion.

Praeger slumped against the door; almost immediately his coat began to smolder. He backed off, righting himself. All about him bricks were beginning to fall, thumping and cracking into dusty chips at his feet.

Eyes watering, heaving within his chest, he stood still for a moment. Waves of heat blasted his face. He stepped into a wash of sunlight, took a breath, and limped away unnoticed—north toward Guinness Village, toward Michele, toward mountains. . . .